JANE AUSTEN

POCKET
GIANTS

JANE AUSTEN

POCKET
GIANTS

CAROLINE
SANDERSON

The
History
Press

First published 2014

The History Press
The Mill, Brimscombe Port
Stroud, Gloucestershire, GL5 2QG
www.thehistorypress.co.uk

British Library Cataloguing in Publication Data.
A catalogue record for this book is available from the British Library.

ISBN 978 0 7524 9319 0

Typesetting and origination by The History Press
Printed in Europe

Contents

There's Something About Jane

These boo-words, 'insular', 'parochial' and 'domestic' could be used against Jane Austen – and have been used on occasion. But she was a great writer. It is easy to mistake what is exotic and unfamiliar for real originality.

David Lodge, 1999[1]

Jane Austen died aged only 41, didn't marry, never had children and lived out her days in the south of England, rarely straying from the genteel and orthodox social circle into which she was born. She completed only six full-length novels, and tasted only brief and limited fame in her lifetime.

Yet, 200 years after her death, she is one of the world's most revered writers, a literary giant, her life the topic of dozens of biographies, her work the subject of thousands of academic studies. In recent decades, her novels have frequently been adapted for television and film. The internet has spawned countless blogs and websites on which all things Austen are analysed and adored. There are mugs, and tea towels, and t-shirts, and books of Jane Austen quotations, and instructions on just how manners maketh man – and woman – according to her expert word.

Novels have been written in imitation of her own, in tribute to her own and in completion of her own. There are sequels, parodies and eroticised versions of her writings, and, most entertainingly perhaps, contemporary mash-ups, including recent bestseller *Pride and Prejudice and Zombies*, which bears the subtitle, 'The Classic Regency Romance – now with Ultraviolent Zombie Mayhem!' Jane, who was not at all averse to a good parody, and wrote several of her own, would probably have found all this adoring preoccupation with her work highly amusing. As she once wrote:

> I could not sit seriously down to write a serious romance under any other motive than to save my life, and if it were indispensable for me to keep it up and never relax into laughing at myself or other people, I am sure I should be hung before I had finished the first chapter.[2]

In this hyper-connected world, why do we still care so much for her stories, drawn in the far-off days of the late eighteenth and early nineteenth centuries on to such a small canvas, 'the little bit (two inches wide) of ivory on which I work with so fine a brush', as Jane Austen herself once called it. 'You are now collecting our People delightfully, getting them exactly into such a spot as is the delight of my life; 3 or 4 Families in a Country Village is the very thing to work on,' she advised her aspiring novelist niece Anna, in 1814.[3] Her own novels rarely extend beyond these parameters, and the biggest dramas we encounter are broken engagements, sprained 'ancles' and that now quaint social crime: elopement.

Despite the fact that she lived in turbulent times, there are no wars in Jane Austen. Poverty and rural crime, which was all too present even in her limited world, rate scarcely a mention. Her plots can be summarised as: girl meets boy and eventually, after varying obstacles are overcome, they marry.

And yet there's still something about Jane, far beyond the famous romances which are the subject of her novels. Over 200 years after they were written they still capture the complexities of human beings, and the nuances of their relationships, with all their joys, tensions, contradictions and ironies – and they continue to beguile readers the world over.

This spinster novelist with little experience of the wider world, raised on a diet of swooning, unrealistic tales of love and scandal, was a genius at observing and describing ordinary human behaviour. Her narratives are immensely satisfying because of the sophistication of their construction and the precise brilliance of the style with which they are told. Her dialogue never sounds less than true.

Sir Walter Scott, the most popular novelist of his day, was one of the first to recognise Austen's talent in this respect, declaring himself envious of her 'exquisite touch which renders ordinary common-place things and characters interesting from the truth of the description and the sentiment'.[4] Genteel ladies and gentlemen, whose behaviour rarely deviates from acceptable social norms, her characters may be, but as she declares in *Emma*, what Jane Austen understood so well was that 'seldom, very seldom does complete truth belong to any human discourse'.

Scratch the surface of her characters' polite social exchanges and universal, timeless human dilemmas emerge. Is this man all he seems to be? Is my friend true? Am I really in love? Hypochondriacs are annoying. Some girls are very silly. Some men are only out for what they can get. Some women only care about money. Austen's insights into what goes on in the human head and heart beneath the social veneer are second to none. The smallest telling detail – a word, a turn of phrase, a witty aside, a foolish remark, a look, a look away – can reveal the innermost workings of her characters' hearts and minds.

Virginia Woolf once remarked that of all great writers, Jane Austen was 'the most difficult to catch in the act of greatness'.[5] It is her minute attention to detail that makes Austen such a giant of a writer and such a favourite of so many readers. Her novels can be returned to again and again, throughout life, because on each reading they will reveal something new. Read her as a teenager and, despite Jane's own protestations that she couldn't write a 'serious romance' to save her life, her novels present themselves as love stories, where the heroine always gets the right man in the end, but finds out things she needs to know about him and about herself along the way. Read them when older, and perhaps more cynical about life and relationships, and her characters reveal not so much their romantic aspirations but the extent to which property, status, health and wealth preoccupy them.

In short, Jane Austen's stories give her readers a profound sense of her characters' inner lives. So what does her own life story tell us?

1

The Clergyman's Daughter
1775–87

Her fire began with herself.

G.K. Chesterton[6]

Jane Austen's story starts in Steventon, a small and little-known village buried deep in the Hampshire countryside. Even today, in this heritage industry era when the birthplaces of famous writers come with coach parks and souvenir shops, not even the smallest monument commemorates Jane Austen's birth in the green field which marks its location.

The Reverend George Austen and his wife Cassandra had moved to Steventon in 1771 from the parsonage in the nearby village of Deane. Seven years after their marriage in Bath in 1764, they had a growing family of three sons: James, George and Edward. Years later, in his *A Memoir of Jane Austen*, Jane's nephew James Edward Austen-Leigh imagined the scene on the day of the move to Steventon: 'Mrs Austen, who was not then in strong health, performed the short journey on a feather-bed, placed upon some soft articles of furniture in the waggon which held their household goods', for the road was a 'mere cart track, so cut up by deep ruts as to be impassable for a light carriage'.

The rectory at Steventon had been refurbished prior to the Austen family's arrival, but was still somewhat dilapidated. Set among fields some distance from the cottages of the main village, it had two storeys, a latticed porch, dormer attic windows and two projecting wings at the back of the house. There was a large garden with elms and sycamores, a shrubbery, flowerbeds and a vegetable patch, gradually sloping up to a terrace walk and a path which led to the parish church of St Nicholas beyond.

Once settled into life at Steventon, the Austens took steps to supplement the meagre income of a country clergyman by taking in pupils. Four or five boys at a time, from the genteel families of the surrounding area, came to live at the rectory to be tutored in Greek and Latin by Rev. Austen. With the arrival of more Austen offspring in succeeding years, the rectory must have been an exceedingly lively place, full of the high spirits and the energetic play of growing boys. James, George and Edward were soon joined by Henry (born 1771), a first sister, Cassandra (born 1773), and then Francis, known as Frank (born 1774).

Into this animated environment, during the especially cold and hard winter of 1775, a seventh child was born, on 16 December. Jane remained indoors with her mother for some weeks after her birth, tucked up against that Siberian winter, her senses slowly waking up to the surroundings that would provide the boundaries of her world for the first twenty-five years of her life.

Her mother breastfed the new arrival for three months or so, and then baby Jane was sent to live with a woman in the village, probably shortly after her christening in April 1776. There she remained for a year or perhaps even eighteen months, only returning permanently to her family when she could easily be managed at home. This practice – not uncommon for genteel families of the time – seems harsh to our twenty-first-century sensibilities with our notions about the importance of bonding between mother and child. But Mrs Austen would have had precious little time for such 'sentiment'. A busy, no-nonsense clergyman's wife, with six other children, a house and school to run, servants to supervise and livestock to husband, she certainly did not have the time to provide the intense supervision which toddlers require. Employing a village wet nurse-cum-nanny to care for Jane was a highly practical solution, which Mrs Austen probably adopted with few pangs. It is hard to know whether this early separation affected their later relationship: Jane's surviving letters do not give much impression of mother-daughter closeness. At a time when the mortality rate for infants under 5 was still very high, concern for the emotional well-being of her offspring probably came some way down Mrs Austen's list of priorities.

One of Jane's elder brothers had given his mother very definite cause for concern, however. The Austens' second son George was born epileptic and possibly deaf and dumb. From an early age he, too, was sent away to be cared for, but this was a permanent arrangement. His upkeep was paid for by his family throughout his life and he lived to 72 – a much riper age than his youngest sister. It is thought that he lodged with his uncle, Mrs Austen's younger brother, Thomas Leigh, who was also disabled. The Austens were disinclined to agonise about this accident of birth, and George appears to have been more or less written out of the family history. Jane does not mention him in any of her surviving letters.

In a more fortunate turn of fate, the next Austen son, Edward, born the year after George in 1767, was adopted at the age of 16 by a distant but wealthy cousin, Thomas Knight and his wife, thus becoming heir to the grand estate of Godmersham Park in Kent, as well as substantial properties in and around Steventon and elsewhere in Hampshire. Throughout their lives, both Jane and Cassandra made frequent trips to Kent to stay with her brother and the eleven children he brought into the world with his wife Elizabeth.

Though Jane's upbringing was respectably genteel, late eighteenth-century Steventon was no rural idyll. Home to perhaps thirty families, it was regularly cut off for days after bad storms or snow. Many of its inhabitants lived in extreme poverty, exacerbated by disease, bad weather and poor harvests, and so charitable works would have been expected of a clergyman's daughter. Jane itemises her 'charities to the poor' in a letter to Cassandra in December 1798: 'I have given a pair of Worsted stockings to Mary Hutchins, Dame Kew, Mary Steevens & Dame Staples, and a shift to Hannah Staples, and a shawl to Betty Dawkins; amounting in all to about half a guinea.'[7] Rural crime was also rife: the Hampshire archives for 1782, for example, lay bare a catalogue of serious felonies including rape, burglaries, house-breaking, sodomy and bestiality. The murder at birth of illegitimate children was alarmingly common. And highwaymen lurked in the woods in and around Steventon. During the summer of 1793, one such felon succeeded in robbing passing carriages over a period of months before the offer of a large reward for his capture made him leave the district. Not before he had robbed a friend of the Austens, however: Mrs Bramston of Oakley Hall was forced to part with 8 guineas after he threatened to blow her brains out.

For all this rural wrongdoing, Jane had a largely happy and unclouded Hampshire childhood. Her formal education took place mainly at home. She and Cassandra were sent away to school twice: the first time when Jane was only 7 years old, to an establishment in Oxford. The school then moved to Southampton, where troops returning from abroad brought an infectious fever with them. Both sisters became ill – Jane dangerously so – and were brought home to recover. They didn't go back. Later, the sisters spent some time at a school in Reading, but perhaps it proved too expensive, because they were home again for good in a matter of months.

In any case, there were plenty of opportunities for learning in a home that was also a school. The number of boys taken in by Jane's parents was small enough to make it feel more like an extended family than a formal institution, and indeed some of the pupils became lifelong friends of the family. Jane grew up, not only with five brothers around her (a final Austen sibling, Charles, was born in 1779), but lots of other boys as well. The rough and tumble must have been quite something. It's easy to imagine that Jane's early years inspired the passage at the beginning of her novel *Northanger Abbey*, which describes the childhood of her heroine, Catherine Morland. Also the daughter of a clergyman, Catherine is one of ten children, and has three older brothers:

She was fond of all boys' plays, and greatly preferred cricket, not merely to dolls, but to the more heroic enjoyments of infancy … she was moreover noisy and wild, hated confinement and cleanliness, and loved nothing so well in the world as rolling down the green slope at the back of the house.

When she grew out of boys' plays and slope-rolling, Jane continued to enjoy being outdoors and was fond of walking in the countryside around Steventon, even in bad weather. 'I enjoyed the hard black Frosts of last week very much, and one day while they lasted walked to Deane by myself', she wrote in December 1798.[8] Such was the roughness of the roads, that even a prolonged spell of rain could isolate Steventon for days. 'There has been a great deal of rain here for this last fortnight … Steventon lane has its full share of it, & I do not know when I shall be able to get to Deane', lamented Jane, writing in October 1798.[9]

Like their creator, Austen heroines are not easily deterred from cross-country walking. In *Pride and Prejudice* Elizabeth Bennett walks 3 miles to the Bingleys' house to visit her sister Jane who is laid up with a severe chill. She crosses 'field after field at a quick pace, jumping over stiles and springing over puddles with impatient activity', arriving with 'weary ancles, dirty stockings, and a face glowing with all the warmth of exercise'. The imperious Caroline Bingley and her sister Mrs Hurst are all disdain: 'Why must she be scampering about the country because her sister has a cold?' 'Yes, and her petticoat; I hope you saw her petticoat, six inches deep in mud.' Miss Bingley tries to goad Mr Darcy into expressing his disapproval: 'To walk three miles, or four miles, or five miles, or whatever it is, above her ancles in dirt, and alone, quite alone! What could she mean by it? It seems to me to shew an abominable sort of conceited independence, a most country town indifference to decorum.' Darcy retorts that it shows 'an affection for her sister that is very pleasing', adding for good measure his observation that her 'fine eyes' had been brightened by the exercise.

The Austen family also had a wide circle of friends and acquaintances among the families who resided in the manor houses and rectories of the neighbouring towns and villages. As a young woman, Jane was frequently invited to balls and supper parties in the great houses and assembly rooms of the district. In his *A Memoir of Jane Austen*, published in 1870, James Edward Austen-Leigh recorded that:

There must have been more dancing throughout the country in those days than there is now. Many country towns had a monthly ball throughout the winter, in some of which the same apartment served for dancing and tea-room. Dinner parties more frequently ended with an extempore dance on the carpet, to the music of a harpsichord in the house, or a fiddle from the village.

In her frequent letters to her sister Cassandra, written whenever the two of them were apart, Jane described many such gatherings, keen to keep her sister up to date with all the local gossip. Here she is in December 1798 reporting with relish on a recent ball: 'There were twenty Dances & I danced them all & without any fatigue … in cold weather & with few couples I fancy I could just as well dance for a week together as for half an hour.'[10] A few weeks later, in January 1799, she attended a ball at nearby Kempshott Park:

I wore my Green shoes last night and took my white fan with me … There was one Gentleman, an officer of the Cheshire, a very good looking Man who I was told very much wanted to be introduced to me; – but as he did not want it quite enough to take much trouble in effecting it, We never could bring it about.[11]

The image of a sociable young woman of considerable energy and animation, plus a sharp sense of humour, emerges from these letters, together with a strong hint of the tone that would characterise her novels.

Jane is at her astringent best in a letter of November 1800, describing a grand ball at Hurstbourne Park, near Whitchurch. Hurstbourne was the home of the Earl of Portsmouth, a former pupil of her father's, who was later declared insane. 'I believe I drank too much wine last night,' she begins, before proceeding to describe some of her fellow guests. 'Mrs Blount … appeared exactly as she did in September with the same broad face, diamond bandeau, white shoes, pink husband, & fat neck.' 'The

Miss Maitlands are both prettyish … with brown skins, large dark eyes, & a good deal of nose … Miss Debary, Susan and Sally made their appearance … and I was as civil to them as their bad breath would allow.'[12] A contender for her most caustic comment came in a letter to Cassandra from Steventon in October 1798: 'Mrs Hall of Sherbourn was brought to bed yesterday of a dead child, some weeks before she expected, "oweing to a fright". I suppose she happened unawares to look at her husband.'[13]

These wickedly witty letters confirm that there was nothing prim or pious about Jane's upbringing as the daughter of a clergyman. In fact, her father, to whom she was close, seems to have been rather liberal and indulgent by the standards of the day. When Jane was young he even allowed her to scribble in the parish registers kept in the church. On forms for the publication of banns of marriage Jane made up three entries in which she tried on for size the names of imaginary prospective husbands: 'The banns of marriage between Henry Frederic Howard Fitzwilliam of London and Jane Austen of Steventon.' 'Edmund Arthur William Mortimer of Liverpool and Jane Austen of Steventon were married in this church.' 'This marriage was solemnized by us, by Jack Smith & Jane Smith, late Austen.' ('A Mrs Smith!' as Sir Walter Elliot in *Persuasion* would have sneered.) In the event, Jane was to keep the name of Austen for the rest of her life.

The Austen household was a bookish one, and Rev. Austen allowed his young daughter – who could read well from the age of 8 – to read any book that took her fancy from among his extensive library of 500 volumes. As a consequence, Jane's early reading was eclectic, encompassing history, poetry, books in French and all the popular novels of the day, many of which contained extremely racy subject matter. Drunkenness, rapes, murders, elopements, adulterous liaisons and bigamous marriages are all common in eighteenth-century fiction. Writing in 1817, the year of Jane's death, her favourite brother Henry recalled, 'It is difficult to say at what age she was not intimately acquainted with the merits and defects of the best essays and novels in the English language.'[14] At a formative age, Jane lapped up the novels of Henry Fielding, Daniel Defoe, Jonathan Swift, Samuel Johnson, Oliver Goldsmith, Fanny Burney, Laurence Sterne and Ann Radcliffe. Samuel Richardson was one of her preferred writers. His sprawling novel *Sir Charles Grandison* was allegedly her favourite. The ghastly flibbertigibbet Isabella Thorpe in *Northanger Abbey* calls it 'an amazing horrid book', so Jane must have liked it.

Despite an abiding love of poetry (William Cowper was a particularly favourite), novels were the preferred reading matter both for Jane and for the whole Austen family, which was clever and learned without having intellectual pretensions. When, in 1798, Jane received a note from a Mrs Martin asking her to become a subscriber to her new lending library, she commented in a letter to Cassandra: 'Mrs Martin tells us that her Collection is not to consist only of Novels, but of every kind of Literature … She might have spared this pretension to our family who are great Novel-readers & not ashamed of being so.'[15] In her own novels, she would often have her less endearing characters damn themselves by proclaiming that they never read novels. There is John Thorpe in *Northanger Abbey*: 'Oh Lord! Not I; I never read novels; I have something else to do … they are the stupidest things in creation.' (By contrast, the novel's hero, Henry Tilney, declares, 'The person, gentleman or lady who has not pleasure in a good novel must be intolerably stupid.') In *Pride and Prejudice* it is Mr Collins who protests that he never reads novels, remarking, 'I have often observed how little young ladies are interested by books of a serious stamp.' In *Persuasion*, the sister of the heroine Anne Elliot, the snobbish Elizabeth, returns a book to Lady Russell unread: 'You may as well take back that tiresome book she would lend me, and pretend I have read it through. I really cannot be plaguing myself for ever with all the new poems and states of the nation that come out. Lady Russell quite bores one with her new publications.' And in *Mansfield Park*, whilst Fanny Price has been a collector of books 'from the first hour of her commanding a shilling', her suitor, Henry Crawford, has the ability to perform speeches from Shakespeare well, but hasn't actually read any of the plays. He is all show, as events will later prove. Unlike Fanny's uneducated sister Susan, no one could ever say of the Austen family that 'the early habit of reading was wanting'.

Neither was the habit of writing. Jane's mother had written light-hearted verse from her youth. Jane's eldest brother James fancied himself as a serious poet, and was also fond of putting on theatricals with his brothers in the barn across the road from the rectory, for which he penned his own prologues. With his brother Henry, he also founded a literary magazine, *The Loiterer*, to which the teenage Jane may have contributed.

The liveliness of Jane's childhood and her wide-ranging early reading helped form her into an exceptionally talented and imaginative young woman who loved to commit the witty compositions of her animated mind to paper. And so, in a small Hampshire village the would-be novelist began to write and an extraordinary life in literature began. In his *A Memoir of Jane Austen*, James Edward writes of Steventon: 'This was the residence of Jane Austen for twenty-five years. This was the cradle of her genius … In strolls along these wood-walks, thick-coming fancies rose in her mind, and gradually assumed the forms in which they came forth to the world.'[16]

Or perhaps Steventon had very little to do with it. Perhaps it was just as the writer and devout Jane Austen fan G.K. Chesterton later put it. Austen was not, he said, 'inflamed or inspired or even moved to be a genius; she simply was a genius. Her fire … began with herself; like the fire of the first man who rubbed two dry sticks together.'[17]

2

The Aspiring Writer
1787–1800

She must have known that, however brilliant or successful her brothers, it was she who had genius.

P.D. James, 1999[18]

The young writer in Jane Austen was fired by her close, lively and intellectually encouraging family. Between the ages of 12 and 16 she wrote skits, plays and stories which she copied into three vellum quarto notebooks with the tongue-in-cheek titles of 'Volume the First', 'Volume the Second' and 'Volume the Third'. The notebooks (now available to view online thanks to a British Library and Bodleian Library project) were crammed with her forward-sloping handwriting, giving the impression of someone who wrote quickly and fluently, but with the frequent crossings-out and amendments of a writer already adept at editing and revising her work. The notebook that contains 'Volume the Second' was a gift from her father and she inscribed it accordingly '*Ex Dono Mei Patris*'. Rev. Austen may also have provided 'Volume the Third'. Inside that one she wrote: 'Effusions of Fancy by a very Young Lady Consisting of Tales in a Style entirely new.'

Jane's teenage compositions were prodigious for her young age and deliciously droll, and they remain great fun to read today. She takes particular pleasure in satirising the overblown romantic fiction of the day. *Love and Freindship* (*sic*), written in 1790, is a short epistolary novel, full of ridiculous coincidences, women who faint repeatedly and girls who disobey their parents. 'Where in the name of wonder did you pick up this unmeaning gibberish? You have been studying novels I suspect,' says one character. In *Lesley Castle*, composed in the early part of 1792 when Jane was 16, there are more comic capers. The fiancé of Charlotte Lutterell's sister Eloisa is thrown from his horse and their impending wedding has to be called off, much to Charlotte's chagrin. She has spent days preparing the wedding breakfast, only to have the 'mortification of finding that I had been Roasting, Broiling and Stewing both the Meat and Myself to no purpose'. Despite the death of the prospective bridegroom, the family gets stuck into the food in an attempt to clear the pantry.

In 1791, Jane wrote an entertainingly opinionated tongue-in-cheek history of England, commissioning charming little medallion-shaped caricatures from her sister Cassandra to illustrate it. On the title page, she described it as: 'The History of England from the reign of Henry the 4th to the death of Charles the 1st. By a partial, prejudiced, & ignorant Historian … NB. There will be very few Dates in this History.' Of Henry VI she wrote:

This King married Margaret of Anjou, a Woman whose distresses & misfortunes were so great as almost to make me who hate her, pity her. It was in this reign that Joan of Arc lived & made such a row among the English. They should not have burnt her – but they did.

Her history is also full of family in-jokes, including a reference to her brother Frank who had by this time joined the Royal Navy. Of Francis Drake, she wrote that 'great as he was, & justly celebrated as a Sailor, I cannot help foreseeing that he will be equalled in this or the next Century by one who tho' now but young, already promises to answer all the ardent & sanguine expectations of his Relations & Friends.'

Early on, Jane adopted the habit of reading her work aloud to her family and close friends, a practice which was to continue with her novels. But by the early 1790s Jane's hitherto close-knit family life was changing fast. Jane, Cassandra and their parents were soon rattling around the once full rectory at Steventon as, one by one, the brothers flew the nest. Frank left home at the age of 15 to join the navy. He went away to sea and did not see his family again for five years. Jane's eldest brother James had long since departed, having gone up to St John's College, Oxford, at the age of 14, when Jane was still only a small child. After being ordained, he became curate at Overton, just 3 miles from Steventon, and in 1792 he married

Anne Mathew, the granddaughter of a duke. In the early 1780s, at the age of 16, Edward had departed to live with his adoptive parents, Mr and Mrs Knight, to be groomed for the life of a country gentleman. By the early 1790s he had settled into his Kent estates and married Elizabeth Bridges, the daughter of a baronet. The first of their eleven children, Fanny, was born in 1793 and became Jane Austen's favourite among her many future nieces and nephews. Jane's favourite brother, Henry, had also attended St John's, Oxford, and planned to be ordained like James. But when war broke out between England and France in early 1793 he abandoned the idea of becoming a clergyman and signed up with the Oxford militia instead.

Among the frequent visitors to Steventon during this time was Jane's exotic cousin Eliza, daughter of Rev. Austen's elder sister Philadelphia. Born in India in 1761, Eliza had spent much of her young life abroad and in 1781 had married a French aristocrat, Count Jean Francois Capot de Feuillide, with whom she had a young son, Hastings. Her stories of the wider world must have entranced the young Jane, who dedicated *Love and Freindship* to her glamorous cousin. In 1794, during the Terror which followed the French Revolution, Eliza's husband was arrested and guillotined. Jane Austen is often taken to task for not mentioning any of the turbulent events in the wider world in her novels. Whatever her reasons for not doing so, in her own life they must have been all too real. Apart from the cruel fate that befell Cousin Eliza's husband, Jane had two brothers enduring danger and hardship on active service during the Napoleonic Wars, for in 1791, at the age of 12, her youngest brother Charles had also joined the navy. Their news, from far-distant ports in a time of war, was often agonisingly slow to arrive. On 24 January 1809, Jane writes of having just received a letter from Charles sent from Bermuda early the previous December.

By the time of her nineteenth birthday in 1794, when her ever-encouraging father made her a present of a small mahogany writing desk, Jane had completed another short epistolary novel entitled *Lady Susan*. Carefully plotted and with fully rounded characters, it was more polished than anything she had yet written. The title character, Lady Susan Vernon, is a beautiful but callous, gold-digging widow who takes pleasure in ensnaring both single and married men whilst trying to force her teenage daughter, Frederica, into marrying a man she does not love. Once she had finished *Lady Susan*, Jane set the story aside and, although she made a copy of it ten years or so later, it was not published until 1871, several decades after her death.

The following year, 1795, Jane composed an early version of *Sense and Sensibility*, the first of her six major novels. Originally called *Elinor and Marianne*, it too started life as a novel in letters, and was the tale of two sisters of contrasting characters: the elder rational and sensible, the younger impulsive, sensitive and full of romantic notions. The novel charts their unsmooth courses towards finding love with their future husbands.

Though there is nothing to suggest that Jane drew on the lives of her own sister and herself for the novel, there were developments in both girls' romantic lives around this time. In 1792, Cassandra had become engaged to Tom Fowle, an impoverished curate in Wiltshire and a former Steventon pupil of Rev. Austen. Neither having any money, they delayed any thought of getting married until Tom's future prospects had improved. In 1795 he was offered a position as chaplain to a regiment which was sailing for the West Indies to fight the French. Promised a good living by the colonel of the regiment once the expedition was over, Tom accepted willingly. Before he left the country that October, he made his will, leaving £1,000 to his fiancée.

During the Christmas of 1795, Cassandra was away from home, staying with her future in-laws in Berkshire. It was at this point that Jane got to know a Tom of her own and embarked on her first serious flirtation. The rectory in the nearby village of Ashe was home to Anne Lefroy, a great friend – and something of a mentor – to the young Jane. Her earliest surviving letters date from the period when Madame (as she was known) Lefroy's nephew, Tom, was staying at Ashe in 1796. 'He is a very gentlemanlike, good-looking, pleasant young man ... he has but one fault ... it is that his morning coat is a great deal too light,' jokes Jane in a letter to her sister.[19] A few days later, she writes, 'I mean to confine myself in future to Mr Tom Lefroy, for whom I do not [*sic*] care sixpence.'[20] A friendship, and perhaps more, had been kindled.

Within days, however, Tom left Hampshire and Jane never saw him again. She wrote to Cassandra: 'At length the Day is come when I am to flirt my last with Tom Lefroy, & when you receive this it will be over – My tears flow as I write, at the melancholy idea.'[21] There was clearly a spark between them. But Jane's letter is so light-hearted in tone, it is impossible to know whether she was seriously attached or not. Some biographers think that the unsuitability of the match – Jane having so little money – led Tom's relatives to separate the two of them deliberately. This may have been the case, but there is little hard evidence that the sudden termination of their relationship had any lasting effect on Jane.

The 2007 film *Becoming Jane*, starring Anne Hathaway and James McAvoy, is, however, based on the notion that Jane was a romantic, inspired to write her greatest works by her thwarted love affair with Tom Lefroy. Quoted in *The Times* when the film came out, Tom's first cousin four times removed, Mrs Helen Lefroy, scoffed at the idea: 'What people don't wish to note is that after he met Jane, he became engaged to the sister of his college friend ...

a simple, biddable girl. People of his ability didn't want intellectuals. He wanted a housekeeper.' By the time Tom Lefroy left Hampshire for good in early 1796, Jane had finished writing *Elinor and Marianne*. The composition of *First Impressions* – the book that was to become her best-loved novel *Pride and Prejudice* – would soon be under way. Far from being a simple, biddable girl, Jane was already demonstrating that she was a fiercely intelligent, talented young woman. And already in thrall to her one true love: writing.

Written in around ten months in 1796 and 1797, *First Impressions*, like *Elinor and Marianne*, has the story of two sisters – Jane and Elizabeth Bennet – at its heart. Elizabeth Bennet is not Jane Austen, but they share the same wit, sparkle and intelligence, and both love to poke fun. 'Follies and nonsense, whims and inconsistencies do divert me, I own, and I laugh at them whenever I can,' says Elizabeth. For many, she is Jane's most wholly attractive character, her only fault a youthful predilection for impulsively judging people on how they first appear, as the novel's original title suggests. Yet Elizabeth also understands – just as Jane herself must have understood – what is at stake if she makes an error and marries the wrong man, or if she fails to marry at all.

Once *First Impressions* was completed, Jane shared the novel with members of her family. It may well have helped to console Cassandra, who was mourning the death of her fiancé, Tom Fowle. Due home from St Domingo (now Haiti) in the Caribbean in the spring of 1797, the news of his demise from a fever arrived instead. Cassandra remained unmarried for the rest of her long life. Other marriages did take place that year, however. After the death of his first wife, Anne, two years previously (leaving him with a 2-year-old daughter, Anna) Jane's brother James married Mary Lloyd, a long-standing friend of the Austen family. And in a rather more surprising match, Henry married his cousin, the widowed Countess Eliza de Feuillide.

Everyone loved *First Impressions*. Jane's father was so taken with it that he decided to try to get it published. In November he wrote to Thomas Cadell, a well-known London publisher whose firm had recently published Fanny Burney's novel *Camilla*, offering them 'a Manuscript Novel, comprised in three Vols' but giving no other details. His offer was declined by return of post, and so, for the time being, *First Impressions* stayed in Steventon where it continued to entertain Jane's family. In January 1799 Jane wrote to Cassandra whilst staying with their brother Edward in Kent: 'I do not wonder at your wanting to read *First Impressions* again, so seldom as you have gone through it, & that so long ago.'[22] Her playful tone suggests that her sister had loved it enough to have read it many times already.

Perhaps because she received such a warm response from those closest to her, Jane was undeterred by her father's failure to interest a publisher in *First Impressions*. She put the book aside and decided to revise the manuscript of *Elinor and Marianne* instead, turning it from a novel in letters into a straight narrative and retitling it *Sense and Sensibility*. In the summer of 1798, Jane travelled to Kent with her parents to visit Edward, who had recently succeeded to the Knight estates and was now living in the very grand Godmersham house, midway between Ashford and Canterbury. During her stay, Jane continued to work on *Sense and Sensibility*, and also hatched an idea for a new novel. Entitled *Susan* (and later to become *Northanger Abbey*), it was a roundly entertaining parody of the Gothic novels of the day, in which the young heroine lets her imagination run away with her to comic effect. It would have had amusing resonance for contemporary readers familiar with the 'horrid' works of novelists like Ann Radcliffe, whose *The Mysteries of Udolpho* was a popular sensation on its publication in 1794. Jane finished writing *Susan* in the summer of 1799.

And so the nineteenth century dawned. George III was on the throne. William Pitt the Younger was Prime Minister. Napoleon Bonaparte had just seized power in France. All Jane's brothers had left home, and she had a growing brood of nephews and nieces. Now in their mid-twenties, both she and Cassandra remained unmarried, but there was still every prospect that they would find husbands.

An unfinished sketch by Cassandra, now in the National Portrait Gallery (the only authenticated version, although there are now a couple of other claimants), shows Jane as an alert young woman with dark brown curling hair and dark, expressive eyes. The reminiscences of her family attest to her charms. 'In person she was very attractive; her figure was rather tall and slender, her step light and firm, and her whole appearance expressive of health and animation,' wrote James Edward Austen-Leigh in his *A Memoir of Jane Austen*. In her *My Aunt Jane: A Memoir*, written in 1867, his sister Caroline Austen recalled their aunt's as 'the first face I can remember thinking pretty'.

At least one firm offer of marriage did later come Jane's way. But in the early nineteenth century, the chances of finding a husband she could not only love, but who would also allow her the freedom to write and give full flow to her genius, were slim indeed. How Jane really felt about remaining single and childless at this stage of her life is difficult to imagine. Her days as a published novelist were still a long way off. But it must still have been with a sense of some satisfaction that she entered the new century with three full-length and, by any standards, accomplished novels to her credit. The would-be writer had fledged into a novelist of great promise.

Within months, however, a major upheaval would bring this productive period to a sudden end. It was to be over ten years before Jane Austen completed another novel.

3

The Social Observer 1800–06

Do you remember Miss Austen's 'Persuasion' with all the streets and scenes in Bath? It was always my favourite.

Beatrix Potter, 1905[23]

Biographical tradition has it that in December 1800, when Mrs Austen told her daughters out of the blue that, within a matter of weeks, she and Rev. Austen planned to leave Steventon for good and retire to Bath, Jane 'fainted away' in shock.

This seems far-fetched. After all, this is the woman who had comprehensively lampooned the whole swooning business in her short early novel, *Love and Freindship*. Its heroine, Laura, records the cautionary tale of her own life in letters to her friend's daughter Marianne: 'Beware of fainting-fits ... Though at the time they may be refreshing and agreable [*sic*] yet beleive [*sic*] me they will in the end, if too often repeated and at improper seasons, prove destructive to your Constitution ... Run mad as often as you chuse; but do not faint.'

The contrast between familiar rural life in a remote Hampshire village and the social whirl of fashionable Bath could not have been greater. So it is perhaps understandable that so many accounts of Jane's life promote the idea that the move was a distressing one. But Jane's surviving letters from her last few years in Steventon suggest that it may actually have been a welcome development for a writer with ambitions. Her social circle had long been composed of the same people, year in, year out, and increasingly waspish comments in her letters about Hampshire society may betray the fact that she was becoming creatively frustrated with the insularity of country life. Perhaps she longed to broaden her horizons and find new inspirations and fresh material. 'It is not difficult to imagine the dreariness of long winter nights in deep country, with no entertainment in the ramshackle rectory except what the four of them could provide for each other,' writes Nigel Nicolson in his 2002 lecture. 'Was Jane Happy in Bath?'[24]

The prospect of leaving for good the only home you have ever known is bound to produce some feelings of apprehension, even at the advanced age of 25. But the move to Bath was hardly a voyage into the unknown for Jane. She had already visited the city several times, and for her mother and father, now aged 61 and 69, spending their retirement in Bath – the city where they had married – may have been a long-standing intention. Even if it came as a blow to her initially, within weeks Jane was making light of the move: 'We plan having a steady Cook, & a young giddy Housemaid, with a sedate, middle aged Man who is to undertake the double office of Husband to the former & sweetheart to the latter.'[25] Reflecting more seriously on leaving Steventon, she wrote significantly: 'We have lived long enough in this Neighbourhood … It must not be generally known that I am not sacrificing a great deal in quitting the Country – or I can expect to inspire no tenderness, no interest in those we leave behind.'[26]

Bath is an important location in several of Jane's novels. Her first visit there probably took place in November 1797. None of her correspondence from this period survives, but the visit is referred to in later letters. It seems likely that Jane stayed with her mother's wealthy, gout-ridden brother, Mr James Leigh-Perrot, and his wife Jane, who spent at least half the year in Bath at their grand address of No. 1 The Paragon. Whatever Jane got up to during this first visit, it must have furnished her with some good material, for she began writing *Susan* shortly afterwards. Published much later as *Northanger Abbey*, the first half of the novel is set in the city. Bath receives at least a mention in Jane Austen's other four major novels. In *Pride and Prejudice*, Wickham goes off there to enjoy himself and get away from his all too hasty marriage to Lydia Bennet. In *Emma*, soon after his proposal to Emma is rebuffed, it is in Bath that Mr Elton finds a wife in the enticing shape of Miss Augusta Hawkins – with an income of £10,000 a year. And a large portion of the action in Jane's last completed novel *Persuasion* also takes place in Bath, including the moving denouement.

From a small provincial town of 3,000 people, confined within higgledy-piggledy medieval lines, Bath had been transformed, within a few decades of the eighteenth century, into England's most fashionable watering hole, and a town second only to London in cultural importance. By the end of the century its population had swelled to 30,000. The prime attraction was its three thermal springs, which rise to the surface through faults in the Mendip rocks. These waters had been known to the Romans, who built a luxurious health resort around them, as *Aquae Sulis*, and they were still in use in medieval times when the most favoured of the three springs, the one closest to Bath Abbey, became known as the King's Spring, after King Henry I. The waters were still famed for their supposed curative powers six centuries later, as eighteenth-century developers sought to capitalise on their potential to attract wealthy visitors.

A sojourn in Georgian Bath wasn't just about taking the waters, of course. As Mrs Allen in *Northanger Abbey* remarks to Henry Tilney: 'Well sir, and I dare say you are not sorry to be back again for it is just the place for young people – and for everybody else too.' Mr Allen has been 'ordered to Bath for the benefit of a gouty constitution'. His intention is to take the waters, leaving Mrs Allen and Catherine Morland free to enjoy 'all the difficulties and dangers of a six week residence in Bath'. For those accompanying relatives not incapacitated by ill health, a stay in bustling Bath encompassed shopping, dancing, promenading, theatre-going and, above all, watching people and gossiping about them.

In the spring of 1799, Jane was just such an accompanying relative. Edward, her wealthy brother from Kent, was suffering from a bout of ill health which had troubled him all through the previous winter. Jane had been less than sympathetic, remarking somewhat drily in a letter to Cassandra the previous December, 'Poor Edward! It is very hard that he who has everything else in the World that he can wish for, should not have good health too.'[27] Edward was advised by his doctors to see what the curative waters of Bath might do for him, so, together with his wife Elizabeth and their two eldest children Fanny and Edward (three younger boys, George, Henry and William, were left behind in Kent), he travelled to Bath, stopping off at Steventon to pick up his mother and younger sister on the way.

The Austen party rented a house at No. 13 Queen Square for six weeks in May and June. *The Bath Chronicle*, which each week announced the latest prominent people to take up residence in the city, recorded in the issue of Thursday 23 May 1799, the arrival of a 'Mr & Mrs E. Austin' (*sic*). Presumably Miss J. Austen, as their poor relation, did not merit a mention. As soon as she arrived at the Queen Square house, Jane sat down to write to Cassandra: 'Well, here we are at Bath; we got here at about one o'clock & have been arrived just long enough to go over the whole house, fix on our rooms, & be very well pleased with the whole of it.'[28]

Built in the Palladian style, Queen Square was among the first new developments in Bath to be designed by John Wood the Elder, one of the primary architects of the Georgian city. On its completion in 1735, the square was the height of fashion. But by 1799, with all the newer developments that had been built to the north and east of Bath, it was no longer quite *the* place to stay. Jane Austen does not appear to have minded: 'I like our situation very much – it is far more chearful than Paragon.'[29] Mrs Austen agreed: a couple of years later, when the Austens were house-hunting in 1801, Jane wrote, 'My mother hankers after the Square dreadfully.'[30] This did not prevent Jane from being satirically aware of the signals that the location of one's lodgings sent out. In *Persuasion* the Misses Musgrove remark, 'I hope we shall be in Bath in the winter; but remember Papa, if we do go, we must be in a good situation – none of your Queen Squares for us!'

It is unclear whether Edward Austen's stay in Bath had a beneficial effect on his health or not. He regularly took the waters, and Jane reported to Cassandra after three weeks or so that 'Edward has been pretty well for this last week, and as the waters have never disagreed with him in any respect, we are inclined to hope that he will derive advantage from them in the end'.[31] But then, a week later, she writes that he has 'not been well these last two days; his appetite has failed him, & he has complained of sick and uncomfortable feelings, which with other symptoms make us think of the Gout'. An apothecary he consults later attributes the problem to 'his having ate something unsuited to his stomach'.[32] Edward's ailments did not, however, prevent him from buying a new pair of coach horses before the end of his stay.

Two years later, Jane Austen and her mother arrived in Bath to go house-hunting. In early January 1801, in a letter to Cassandra, Jane had discussed the pros and cons of various locations in the city: 'We know that Mrs Perrot will want to get us into Axford Buildings, but we all unite in particular dislike of that part of the Town & therefore hope to escape.'[33] Axford Buildings was very close to the Paragon, and it is clear that Jane did not always get on with her aunt. 'I flatter myself that our apartment will be one of the most complete things of the sort all over Bath – Bristol included,' she added cheerfully. The winter season was over, which must have increased the number of properties on offer. 'Bath is getting so very empty that I am not afraid of doing too little,' wrote Jane in May.[34] Still, her letters detail a busy round of parties and social gatherings throughout that month, as the search for a suitable house continued. Cassandra and her father joined them in Bath shortly afterwards. Then there is a three-year silence. No more letters survive until September

1804, when Jane wrote to Cassandra whilst on holiday at Lyme Regis.

The Austens eventually decided on a house at No. 4 Sydney Place, opposite the present-day Holborne Museum. On 21 May 1801, an advertisement had appeared in *The Bath Chronicle* for a lease of three and a quarter years on the property: 'The situation is desirable, the Rent very low and the Landlord is bound by Contract to paint the first two floors this summer.' Having taken the house, the Austens went off on holiday to Sidmouth in Devon, to allow the necessary redecoration to take place.

Jane Austen's knowledge of Bath made her adept at choosing locations in the city to suit her characters. This is particularly true of the addresses she selects in *Persuasion*, which has snobbery as one of its prevailing themes. Her heroine, Anne Elliot, pays regular visits to an old school friend, Mrs Smith, who, crippled with rheumatic fever, is lodging in a 'very humble way' in Westgate Buildings, in the lower part of the city, within carrying distance of the Cross Bath. Anne's horribly snobbish father, Sir Walter Elliot, is most put out when he discovers that his daughter is deigning to frequent such a place (and to visit 'a mere Smith' at that): 'Westgate Buildings! … and who is a Miss Anne Elliot to be visiting in Westgate Buildings? A Mrs Smith! Westgate Buildings must have been rather surprised by the appearance of a carriage drawn up near its pavement.' On a later visit, no carriage is available, so Anne makes the long downhill walk from her grand lodgings in Camden Place to Westgate Buildings. She doesn't mind because it gives her the opportunity to muse on 'high-wrought love and eternal constancy'.

Anne, still a spinster at the age of 27, has sacrificed a great deal by staying faithful to Captain Wentworth, the only man she has ever loved. Eight years previously, a close family friend had persuaded her to break off her engagement to him, in the belief that he wasn't good enough for the daughter of a baronet. Anne has never ceased to regret her decision: 'Her attachment and regrets, had for a long time, clouded every enjoyment of youth; and an early loss of bloom and spirits had been their lasting effect.'

In November 1802, when she too was approaching an unmarried 27, Jane left Bath with Cassandra to visit their childhood friends, Elizabeth, Alethea and Catherine Bigg, at Manydown House near Basingstoke in Hampshire. During their stay, the Bigg sisters' younger brother Harris made a proposal of marriage to Jane. She accepted, and the whole household went to bed rejoicing at such a suitable match. The next morning, after a sleepless night, Jane decided she had made a mistake and declined his proposal. She and Cassandra left Hampshire under a cloud and returned to Bath.

Harris Bigg-Wither was the heir to a considerable estate. Had she married him, Jane would have become mistress of a large Hampshire house close to her birthplace and could have assured the comfort of her parents and sister for the rest of their lives. This makes it understandable that she succumbed to temptation, if only for one night. She did not love Harris Bigg-Wither, but that was not an insurmountable hurdle. After all, another 27-year-old, Charlotte Lucas, had embraced a worse fate in engaging herself to Mr Collins in *Pride and Prejudice* ('I am not romantic you know. I never was. I ask only a comfortable home.') Perhaps what Jane Austen could not bear to give up was the freedom to write. For this, she was prepared to forsake her last chance of a suitable marriage. As biographer Claire Tomalin puts it in *Jane Austen: A Life*: 'We would naturally rather have *Mansfield Park* and *Emma* than the Bigg-Wither baby she might have given the world, and who would almost certainly have prevented her from writing any further books.'

Was Jane happy in Bath? The popular consensus seems to be that she hated the place. The evidence for this seems to come entirely from the opinions expressed by the characters in her novels, however. In *Persuasion*, Anne Elliot, who spent three years at school in Bath after the death of her mother, is no fan of the place: 'She disliked Bath and did not think it agreed with her.' Little wonder then that, when she arrives for what is to be a lengthy stay, 'she caught the first dim view of the extensive buildings, smoking in rain, without any wish of seeing them better'. This no more reflects Jane Austen's own feelings than the passage in *Northanger Abbey* which describes Catherine's Morland's very different state of mind on getting her own first glimpse of the place: 'Catherine was all eager delight; – her eyes were here, there, every where, as they approached its fine and striking environs, and afterwards drove through those streets which conducted them to the hotel. She was come to be happy, and she felt happy already.' And later: 'Oh! who can ever be tired of Bath?'

It is always dangerous to assume that the pronouncements in Jane Austen's novels convey the real opinions of their author. After all, when narrating *Northanger Abbey* she remarks that 'A woman, especially, if she have the misfortune of knowing any thing, should conceal it as well as she can'. It was advice that she herself was singularly incapable of following.

It seems more sensible to look for evidence of Jane's real feelings about Bath in her own letters, but even this approach has its pitfalls. When she arrived with her mother to begin the search for a permanent home in May 1801, Jane wrote to Cassandra: 'The first veiw [*sic*] in fine weather does not answer my expectations; I think I see more distinctly thro' Rain. – The Sun was got behind everything, and the appearance of the place from the top of Kingsdown Hill was all vapour, shadow, smoke and confusion.'[35] This comment is often cited as evidence of

Jane's dislike of Bath, yet all she really admits is that her first sight of her future home was a bit hazy.

Given the relative glamour of Bath after the sleepiness of Hampshire, it is quite plausible that Jane spent the four years she lived in the city thoroughly enjoying the social scene. A letter written in May 1801 describes a ball she attended with her Uncle and Aunt Leigh Perrot:

> By nine o'clock, my Uncle, Aunt and I entered the rooms & linked Miss Winstone on to us. – Before tea, it was rather a dull affair; but then the beforetea did not last long, for there was only one dance, danced by four couple. – Think of four couple, surrounded by about an hundred people, dancing in the upper rooms at Bath![36]

After tea, Jane and her companions cheered up considerably as 'the breaking up of private Parties sent some scores more to the Ball, and tho' it was shockingly & inhumanely thin for this place, there were people enough I suppose to have made five or six very pretty Basingstoke assemblies'.[37]

The Austens lived in their Sydney Place house from 1801 to 1804, leaving Bath to holiday on the south coast – at Sidmouth in 1801, Dawlish in 1802 and Lyme Regis in 1803 and 1804. By the time of their second stay at Lyme, however, the Austens had moved lodgings in

Bath. Perhaps the rent proved too expensive for their next home was at No. 3 Green Park Buildings East, close to the River Avon. When house-hunting in 1801, they had viewed and dismissed a house in the same location. Despite it being 'so very desirable in size and situation', the 'observations of the damps' and 'reports of discontented families and putrid fevers' led the Austens to reject it. In 1804 something – probably lack of money – forced them to reconsider.

Within three months of their removal to Green Park Buildings, Jane's father was dead. After two days' sudden illness in January 1805, Rev. George Austen 'closed his virtuous and happy life',[38] as Jane put it in a letter to her brother Frank at sea. The lease on their lodgings had another three months to run, so his widow and daughters stayed until it was up. Mrs Austen was in no hurry to leave Bath, despite the fact that money was now a matter of grave concern. The greater part of Rev. Austen's income, which was derived from his parish livings, terminated with his death, leaving his widow and daughters in much reduced circumstances. Jane's brothers rallied round and offered enough financial help to render them comfortable. Even so, their household expenditure had to be pruned. The Austens cut the number of servants they employed from three to one, and were thus able to look for smaller lodgings. They found them at No. 25 Gay Street and had moved there by April 1805.

Though none of Jane's letters from that address survive to explain why, they soon moved again, this time to Trim Street. In 1801 Jane writes that her mother 'will do everything in her power to avoid Trim Street'.[39] Four years later their reduced circumstances meant they could avoid it no longer. Trim Street was cramped and narrow and, unlike bustling Gay Street or elegant Sydney Gardens, it was tucked apologetically away from Bath's fashionable thoroughfares.

Then, in 1806, a move to another town entirely beckoned when Jane's brother Frank invited his mother and sisters to come and live in Southampton. Frank had recently married and thought that his mother and sisters would be good company for his wife Mary during his long absences at sea. It would also give everyone the opportunity to share expenses. And so, on 1 July 1806, after visiting James Austen and his family in Steventon (where James had taken over his father's living as rector) and then various friends and relatives in Gloucestershire, Warwickshire and Staffordshire, the Austen women left Bath for good and settled into a new life in Southampton. After the death of her mother, with whom she had lived for many years, their long-standing Hampshire friend Martha Lloyd, the elder sister of James Austen's second wife Mary, also came to live with them.

On 30 June 1808, whilst staying with her brother Edward at Godmersham, Jane wrote to Cassandra: 'It is two years tomorrow since we left Bath for Clifton – with what happy feelings of escape!'[40] The clinching evidence that she could not wait to get away? Reduced to straitened circumstances and lodged in an insalubrious backwater, it is hardly surprising that it felt like an escape. But this does not mean that Jane did not retain happy memories of her earlier years in Bath – years which were also to inspire the setting for *Persuasion*, one of the three great novels she had yet to write.

During her Bath years, Jane appears to have put down her pen almost completely. Having written almost constantly throughout her teens and early twenties, this is a striking development, and another factor that has led many biographers to believe she was unhappy, even depressed. 'The silence asks questions about the flow of Jane Austen's creative energies, and about her reconciliation to the life she had been handed,' writes novelist Carol Shields in her biography of Jane. But perhaps she was just too busy to write or maybe she lacked the seclusion she needed to match the output of previous years? Her mind was far from idle. And, for the first time since her father's unsuccessful attempt some years before, the family sought to get one of Jane's novels published. Henry delegated one of his business partners to offer the manuscript of *Susan* to a London publisher named Richard Crosby. Crosby agreed to pay £10 for it and promised 'early publication'. Everyone was ecstatic, but then nothing happened. It was another blow to Jane's hopes of becoming a published author.

Nevertheless, in 1803 or 1804, not long after she had turned down Harris Bigg-Wither's proposal, Jane did begin to write something new. Though it was to remain unfinished, *The Watsons* puts the thorny subject of marriage under the spotlight as never before. When the novel opens, its heroine Emma Watson has just returned to the bosom of her genteel but poor birth family after many years away, during which time she has been brought up by a wealthy aunt. The aunt has remarried, depriving Emma of the generous inheritance she once hoped to have. Emma's rediscovered sister Elizabeth speaks movingly of her desperate need to find a husband:

> You know we must marry. – I could do very well single for my own part, – A little company and a pleasant ball now and then, would be enough for me, if one could be young forever, but my father cannot provide for us, and it is very bad to grow old and be poor and laughed at.

In 1806, aged 31, unmarried and entirely dependent on the goodwill of her brothers both for money and for a roof over her head, it looked increasingly as if this could be Jane's fate too. All she had going for her was her writing.

4

The Spinster Aunt
1806–11

All this was done by a quiet maiden lady who had merely pen and ink at her disposal ... Only those who have realized for themselves the ridiculous inadequacy of a straight stick dipped in ink when brought into contact with the rich and tumultuous glow of life can appreciate to the full the wonder of her achievement.

Virginia Woolf, 1913[41]

For the next three years Jane lived a life of frugal but cosy domesticity in her brother's household in Castle Square, Southampton. There were lots of comings and goings. 'When you receive this, our guests will be all gone or going; and I shall be left to the comfortable disposal of my time, to ease of mind from the torments of rice puddings and apple dumplings,' she wrote to Cassandra in January 1807,[42] following the departure of James and family, who had been staying for the New Year. Frank was planning to go skating in the meadows down by the beach, she reported, and they had made some new acquaintances, the Lances. Jane referred, with comic emphasis, to her genteel poverty: 'They live in a handsome style and are rich ... and we gave her to understand that we are far from so; she will soon feel therefore that we are not worth her acquaintance.'[43] A few weeks later, she informed her sister that 'Frank has got a very bad Cough, for an Austen; – but it does not disable him from making a very nice fringe for the Drawingroom – Curtains ... We hear that we are envied our House by many people, & that the Garden is the best in the Town.'[44]

At the time, Cassandra was on an extended stay with Edward in Kent, helping to look after his children and attend to his wife, Elizabeth, who had given birth to another daughter – aptly named Cassandra-Jane – the previous autumn. Both Jane and Cassandra made frequent visits to stay with their brothers, who had growing broods of children (James three and Edward ten), although it seems that Cassandra was more welcome at Godmersham than Jane. In her *Recollections of Aunt Jane*, written in 1864, James' daughter Anna recalled:

> Aunt Jane was generally the favourite with children, but with the young people of Godmersham it was not so. They liked her indeed as a playfellow, & as a teller of stories, but they were not really fond of her. I believe their mother was not; at least she very much preferred the elder sister.[45]

In a letter written years later, Edward's eldest daughter and Jane's favourite niece, Fanny, remembered her aunt Jane as:

> not so refined as she ought to have been from her talent … Both the Aunts were brought up in the most complete ignorance of the World & its ways (I mean as to fashion &c) & if it had not been for Papa's marriage which brought them into Kent

… they would have been, tho' not less clever and agreeable in themselves, very much below par as to good Society and its ways.[46]

During her stays in Kent, Jane's status as a poor relative was thrown into particularly sharp relief. A visiting hairdresser, Mr Hall, charged her sister-in-law Elizabeth the extortionate sum of 5 shillings every time he dressed her hair, 'allowing', wrote Jane, 'nothing for the pleasures of his visit here, for meat, drink & Lodging' and the 'benefit of Country air'. Yet he charged Jane only 2 shillings and 6 pence to cut her hair. 'He certainly respects either our Youth or our poverty,' she joked to Cassandra.[47] In her surviving letters from Godmersham, Jane liked to give the impression – at least on the surface – that she was enjoying all the expensive indulgences her brother's grand country residence provided. 'In another week I shall be at home – & then, my having been at Godmersham will seem like a Dream,' she wrote to Cassandra in 1808.[48] 'In the meantime for Elegance & Ease & Luxury.' During her stay in the June and July of that year, there was an unexpected spell of 'cold, disagreeable weather'. Being Godmersham, no expense was spared as to fires: 'It is now half past Twelve, and having heard Lizzy read, I am now moved down into the Library for the sake of a fire … & here in warm & happy solitude proceed to acknowledge this day's Letter.'[49] Not surprisingly, Godmersham's well-stocked library was Jane's favourite room. During one visit she wrote, 'I am now alone in the Library, Mistress of all I survey … At this present time I have five Tables, Eight & twenty Chairs & two fires all to myself.'[50]

In these spacious surroundings, which must have provided a level of peace and quiet which she could not find at home, Jane got some good work done, writing parts of both *Mansfield Park* and *Emma*. Later, her niece Marianne – Edward Austen's seventh child – recalled that her aunt:

> used to bring the MS of whatever novel she was writing with her, and would shut herself up with my elder sisters in one of the bedrooms to read them aloud. I and the younger ones used to hear peals of laughter through the door, and thought it very hard that we should be shut out from what was so delightful. I also how remember how Aunt Jane would sit quietly working beside the fire in the library, saying nothing for a good while, and then would suddenly burst out laughing, jump up and run across the room to a table where pens and paper were lying, write something down, and then come back to the fire and go on quietly working as before.[51]

Whilst visiting in 1805, Jane struck up a friendship with a member of the Godmersham staff: Fanny's governess,

Miss Anne Sharp. Miss Sharp's time in Kent was relatively short; having arrived early in 1804, she had to resign in the spring of 1806 due to continued ill health. Jane missed her during her subsequent visits. 'Three years ago we were more animated with you and Harriot and Miss Sharp,' she wrote to Cassandra in 1808.[52] Jane sent Miss Sharp copies of her novels (Miss Sharp's favourite was *Pride and Prejudice*) and the two women continued to correspond until Jane's death. Cassandra sent Miss Sharp some small mementos of her sister: a lock of hair and a bodkin which Jane had used regularly for more than twenty years: 'I know how these articles, trifling as they are, will be valued by you & I am very sure that if she is now conscious of what is passing on earth it gives her pleasure they should be so disposed of.'[53]

Anne Sharp led the life of a governess and lady's companion so dreaded by Jane's impoverished female characters like Jane Fairfax in *Emma* and Elizabeth Watson in *The Watsons*. It is interesting that Jane seems to have gravitated more naturally towards Miss Sharp's company than that of the grand but dull representatives of Kent society who came calling and on whom Edward paid an endless round of visits in return. Her descriptions of these people are not flattering: 'I have discovered that Lady Elizabeth for a woman of her age and situation has astonishingly little to say for herself, & that Miss Hatton has not much more.'[54] 'Mrs Britton called here on Saturday

… She is a large, ungenteel Woman, with self-satisfied & would-be elegant manners.'[55] 'We have got rid of Mr R Mascall … I did not like him either. He talks too much & is conceited – besides having a vulgarly shaped mouth.'[56]

The duration of Jane's stays in Kent was also a source of frustration at times. Her letters record occasions when she felt stranded, her travel arrangements completely out of her hands, for, as a single woman, she couldn't go home by public conveyance until her father or one of her brothers was able to take her. Either it was months before a suitable opportunity arose or she was snatched away from Kent far too soon. During her visit in 1796, for example, her plans were thrown into chaos when her brother Frank, who was to take her to stay with her friends, the Pearsons, in London, was recalled to his ship unexpectedly early. Jane could not go with him to town as there was a risk that she would be left stranded with nowhere to stay: 'If the Pearsons were not at home, I should inevitably fall a Sacrifice to the arts of some fat Woman who would make me drunk with Small Beer.'[57] She had to hope instead that her father would come to town to 'fetch home his prodigal Daughter'. In 1808, no sooner had Jane arrived at Godmersham than she was summoned to Edward's study to discuss how she was to get back to Southampton again (she was told she had to leave with Edward when he set off on a business trip to Alton). 'I should have preferred a rather longer stay here certainly,' she reflected, 'but there is not prospect of any later conveyance for me.'[58] There was no possibility either of calling in on cousins in Kent and Surrey on the way as she had hoped to do. 'Till I have a travelling purse of my own, I must submit to such things,' she wrote, resignedly.[59]

And then a family tragedy occurred. On 28 September 1808, 35-year-old Elizabeth Austen gave birth to her eleventh child, Brook-John. As usual, Cassandra was staying at Godmersham at the time, and on 1 October Jane wrote to her sister from Southampton: 'We are extremely glad to hear of the birth of the Child, and trust everything will proceed as well as it begins.'[60] On 10 October, shortly after eating a hearty dinner, Elizabeth was taken ill and died within hours. It was a shattering blow for Edward. Jane pictured her brother at Godmersham, 'restless in Misery going from one room to the other – & perhaps not seldom upstairs to see all that remains of his Elizabeth'.[61]

Death during or following childbirth was common in Jane Austen's time. Even if they survived almost yearly confinements with little medical care, constant pregnancy took its toll on women's minds and bodies. Despite never having children herself, Jane saw plenty of evidence of maternal suffering among her friends and family, such that she was moved to make numerous comments in her letters about husbands needing to learn the meaning of abstinence. Only a week before Elizabeth's death, she responded to reports that Mrs Tilson, the 31-year-old wife of her brother Henry's banking partner was pregnant once more (with her seventh child): 'Poor woman! how can she honestly be breeding again?'[62] 'That Mrs Deedes is to have another Child I suppose I may lament,' she had written from Southampton in 1807.[63] With every new family pregnancy, spinsterhood must have seemed a more attractive state – and certainly the only state in which, as a woman, one could aspire to be a published writer.

Of her writing during this time, Jane says virtually nothing. Despite those occasional bursts of work at Godmersham, perhaps it was still too difficult to find the space and concentration, living in a busy household, subject to frequent visitors and new arrivals. In 1807, Frank Austen's wife Mary gave birth to a daughter, Mary-Jane. Frank and Mary were embarking on family life (they would go on to have another ten children, with Mary sadly destined to die shortly after the birth of her eleventh child, exactly as her sister-in-law Elizabeth had done) and would soon need more space in a home they currently shared with four adult women. So family discussions began about where they might move to next.

This time it was brother Edward who stepped in with a proposal of accommodation. He offered his mother and sisters a choice: a house in Kent close to Godmersham or a move back to Hampshire, where Edward also owned substantial properties. He was the main landowner in the village of Chawton, a mile from the town of Alton, and some 12 miles from Steventon. A house there, known as Chawton Cottage, had became vacant and Edward offered it to his mother and sisters. The Austen women chose Chawton over Kent, and so a move back to Hampshire, the county of her birth, beckoned for Jane. Though money would still be tight, she, her mother, Cassandra and Martha could live rent-free and would automatically become highly respected members of the village community, as befitted the mother and sisters of the local squire.

They must surely have been ecstatic at the idea of a permanent home of their own at last. Jane excitedly mentioned the move to Chawton in a letter to Cassandra as early as October 1808. 'Every body is much acquainted with Chawton & speaks of it as a remarkably pretty village,' she wrote in December 1808.[64] Just as when she had left Steventon eight years before, Jane had high hopes of a livelier existence there too: 'A larger circle of acquaintance & and increase of amusement is quite in character with our approaching removal.'[65]

With a more settled existence at Chawton in prospect, Jane's thoughts returned determinedly to her writing. Galvanised, she wrote a terse letter to Richard Crosby, the publisher who had bought *Susan* from her six years previously. Under the assumed name of Mrs Ashton Dennis, she offered to supply a new copy, 'supposing the MS by some carelessness to have been lost'.[66] She concluded: 'Should no notice be taken of this Address, I shall feel myself at liberty to secure the publication of my work by applying elsewhere.' Crosby wrote back almost by return, acknowledging his purchase of *Susan* but stalling that 'there was not any time stipulated for its publication, neither are we bound to publish it'.[67] Its author could buy back the manuscript if she so wished for £10, the same price as they had paid for it. For a woman who lived on around £50 a year this was far more than Jane could afford, and for the time being she had to let *Susan* go. What she did not let go of, however, was her resolve to start writing again.

5

The Published Novelist
1811–17

You're drawn into the story, and you come out the other end, and you know you've seen something great in action. But you can't see the pyrotechnics; there's nothing flashy.

J.K. Rowling, 2001[68]

Jane, Cassandra, Mrs Austen and Martha moved into their new home in July 1809. Shortly afterwards, Frank's wife Mary gave birth to their second child, a boy, Francis William, and Jane sent some congratulatory verses to her brother which began: 'My dearest Frank, I wish you joy / Of Mary's safety with a Boy.'[69] In the last stanza, she wrote of their new accommodation:

> Our Chawton home, how much we find
> Already in it, to our mind;
> And how convinced, that when complete
> It will all other houses beat
> That ever have been made or mended,
> With rooms concise, or rooms distended.
> You'll find us very snug next year ...

Built in the early eighteenth century, the red-brick Chawton Cottage – a former inn – was a good-sized house. Its six bedrooms provided ample space for the Austens and Martha, and for visiting family – though Jane and Cassandra chose to share a bedroom as they had always done. Outside there was a kitchen garden, a backyard and some outbuildings. Edward had arranged for some work to be done on the house before his mother and sisters moved in, renewing the plumbing and moving a window from the front of the house with its view of the road, to the side, providing a more private aspect over the garden.

Chawton Cottage was situated at an important fork in the turnpike road. Coaches regularly rattled through the village on their way to Alton and London to the north, or back towards Winchester or Gosport to the west and south. Unlike Jane's previous Hampshire home in sleepy Steventon, Chawton Cottage, situated right on the road, was a place where you could sit and watch the world go by. And the world could watch you too. Not long after Jane moved to the cottage, Mrs Knight, her brother Edward's adoptive mother, wrote to her granddaughter Fanny: 'I heard of the Chawton party looking very comfortable at Breakfast, from a gentleman who was travelling by their door in a Post-chaise.'

Life settled into a comfortable and productive routine. Breakfast was taken at around nine o'clock after some of the day's errands and chores were out of the way. It was usually Jane herself who unlocked the cupboard by the fireplace, took out the precious tea (a comparatively expensive commodity in those days), boiled the kettle and prepared a meal of tea, toast and pound cake. Or occasionally she made cocoa. For the rest of the day,

Cassandra took charge of the housekeeping, leaving her sister at liberty to write.

Jane would sit by the dining room window at a small, uneven three-legged table, no more than 3ft high. On it she set her writing desk (probably the same one her father bought for her in 1794) and worked away, quill pen in hand, in full view of the street. The squeaky door into the dining room was left unoiled so that Jane could tell when someone was coming and slide her writings out of sight. 'I have no doubt that I, and my sisters and cousins, in our visits to Chawton, frequently disturbed this mystic process, without having any idea of the mischief we were doing,' wrote Jane's nephew James Edward Austen-Leigh in his *A Memoir of Jane Austen*.

Jane had chosen one of the noisiest rooms in the house in which to write. Along the turnpike road came the coaches, including the local collier's coach, which passed once a day from Alton, drawn by six horses. Farm carts, gigs and occasional grand private carriages added to the traffic. In one of Jane's letters from Chawton she wrote of seeing 'a countless numbers of Postchaises full of Boys pass by yesterday morning – full of future Heroes, Legislators, Fools, & Vilains'.[70] These were schoolboys on their way to Winchester College, the alma mater of James Edward and all Jane's Kent nephews. Yet, amidst all this hubbub, the only thing Jane ever complained about in her letters was the difficulty of concentrating on her work whilst trying to run a household at the same time: 'Composition seems to me Impossible with a head full of Joints of Mutton & doses of Rhubarb.'[71]

Neither three-legged tables nor street noise nor domestic headaches prevented Jane from establishing an extraordinary work rate almost as soon as she moved to Chawton. It was as if, after years of storing up her ideas, the floodgates could finally open. In the summer of 1809 she took out the manuscript of *Sense and Sensibility*, which she had last worked on in 1798. She had already once revised the original novel – written in letter form and entitled *Elinor and Marianne*. Now, more than ten years later, she made some additional small changes in order to update it. Then, undeterred by her previous rejections, she determined on getting it published. In 1810 her brother Henry, who had taken on the role of Jane's literary mentor after their father's death, sent *Sense and Sensibility* to another publisher: Thomas Egerton of Whitehall.

Egerton agreed to publish the book, but only on commission, meaning that the author had both to cover the costs of printing it and contribute towards advertising and distribution costs. Egerton would take a 10 per cent commission on sales, with the author remaining liable for all losses. Henry and his wife Eliza footed the bill and an excited Jane went up to London to stay with them at their smart Sloane Street house in April 1811. In between shopping trips ('I am sorry to tell you that I am getting very extravagant & spending all my Money,' she wrote to Cassandra), walks in Kensington Gardens, trips to the theatre, dinners and other social engagements, Jane worked on the page proofs, assuring Cassandra that she was 'never too busy to think of S&S. I can no more forget it than a mother can forget her sucking child.'[72]

After a nerve-racking delay of some months, *Sense and Sensibility* was finally published in October 1811 as a 'New Novel by a Lady'. At first, only Jane's immediate family members shared the closely guarded secret of her authorship, and her identity remained a mystery to the public. Around 750 copies of the book were printed, with a purchase price of 15 shillings for the three-volume set. It was soon attracting the attention of the chattering classes of the day. Even the 16-year-old heir to the throne, Princess Charlotte, read it, remarking that it 'interested me much'.[73] By the summer of 1813 the book had sold out, making Jane a profit of £140. At last, she was a published writer – albeit anonymous – earning her own money for the first time in her life. Along with the delight of seeing her work in print must have come the delicious sensation that her days of total economic dependency on her brothers were at an end. It was a vindication, too, of everything she had sacrificed – marriage, children and material wealth – in order to write. What a time to savour!

Fifteen months later, in January 1813, *Pride and Prejudice* followed *Sense and Sensibility* into print. Jane 'lopt & cropt' the manuscript, and in the autumn of 1812 Thomas Egerton offered to buy the copyright. Jane agreed, despite the fact that *Sense and Sensiblity* had been published on a commission basis and had therefore earned her royalties. Advice was in short supply, however. Eliza was gravely ill and Henry was preoccupied. This new arrangement with Egerton also meant that no money needed to be paid out in advance. '*Pride & Prejudice* is sold,' wrote Jane to Martha Lloyd. 'Egerton gives £110 for it. – I would rather have had £150, but we could not both be pleased, and I am not at all surprised that he should not chuse to hazard so much.'[74]

Among unsuspecting friends, who had no idea of its author's identity, *Pride and Prejudice* was showing a hint of the vast popularity it would one day enjoy across the world. Mrs Austen and Jane read the first volume to their neighbour Mrs Benn. 'She really does seem to admire Elizabeth,' Jane wrote to her sister. 'I must confess that I think her as delightful a creature as ever appeared in print, & how I shall be able to tolerate those who do not like her at least, I do not know.'[75] Fanny, Jane's favourite niece, who was in on the secret, read *Pride and Prejudice* at Godmersham, and Jane pronounced her praise 'very gratifying': 'Her liking Darcy & Elizabeth is enough. She might hate all the others, if she would.'[76] Among the novel's more celebrated fans was the playwright Richard Brinsley Sheridan, who called it 'one of the cleverest things

[he] ever read'.[77] And Annabella Milbanke, the future wife of Lord Byron, pronounced it 'a very superior work … It depends not on any of the common resources of novel writers, no drownings, no conflagrations, nor runaway horses, nor lap-dogs and parrots, nor chambermaids and milliners, nor rencontres and disguises.'[78]

Jane had a printed copy of *Pride and Prejudice* in her hand by the end of January 1813. 'I want to tell you that I have got my own darling Child from London,' she wrote ecstatically to Cassandra. 'The Advertisement is in our paper to day for the first time; – 18s – He shall ask £1-1 for my two next, & £1-8 for my stupidest of all.'[79]

By this time, Jane had indeed completed her 'next' – *Mansfield Park* – the first novel she had wholly written whilst living at Chawton. The book is something of a tribute to her two sailor brothers, Frank and Charles. In July 1813, Jane wrote to Frank, 'I have something in hand, which I hope on the credit of *P&P* will sell well, tho' not half so entertaining. And by the bye – shall you object to my mentioning the Elephant in it, & two or three other of your old Ships?'[80] The heroine of *Mansfield Park*, Fanny Price, who has a much-loved sailor brother William, is painfully shy and therefore less immediately attractive than Elizabeth Bennet. No one takes much notice of what mouse-like Fanny says because, for long periods, she hardly speaks: 'She was always more inclined to silence when feeling most strongly.' Instead she observes, and what she observes are crucial details which largely pass the other characters by. In the end, events prove Fanny to be wise beyond her years. 'We all have a better guide in ourselves, if we would attend to it, than any other person can be,' she remarks at one point, and that is an important theme of the novel.

Once her first two novels had received a good critical reception Jane seems to have become more relaxed about not remaining anonymous and word spread as to the identity of the author of *Pride and Prejudice*. 'I beleive [*sic*] whenever the 3rd appears, I shall not even attempt to tell Lies about it – I shall rather try to make all the Money than all the Mystery I can of it. People shall pay for their Knowledge if I can make them,' Jane wrote to Cassandra from Godmersham.[81] When he realised his aunt was famous, Jane's nephew James Edward composed the following verse in her honour:

> No words can express, my dear aunt, my surprise
> Or make you conceive how I opened my eyes,
> Like a pig butcher Pile has just struck with a knife,
> When I heard for the very first time in my life
> That I had the honour to have a relation,
> Whose works were dispersed through the whole of
> the nation[82]

The Chawton years continued to be extraordinarily productive. In January 1814, Jane began another novel, to be entitled *Emma*. Her 21-year-old niece, James' daughter Anna, was also writing a novel at around this time. She sent some chapters to her Aunt Jane who read them aloud at home – 'we are all very much amused' – and gave her a few well-chosen bits of advice, among them this famous nugget: 'You are now collecting your People delightfully, getting them exactly into such a spot as is the delight of my life; – 3 or 4 Families in a Country Village is the very thing to work on.'[83] Jane was herself working on just such a scenario in *Emma*.

Mansfield Park was published on 9 May 1814 to very little ado. Jane made up for the lack of reviews by recording the opinions of friends and family. Most were complimentary but their praise was generally more muted than for *Pride and Prejudice*. Her brother Frank said that, although he 'did not think it as a whole equal to P&P', it still had 'many & great beauties'.[84] As a naval man, he was well placed to snigger at Mary Crawford's louche remark about her acquaintance with a 'circle of admirals' in the novel: 'Of Rears and Vices, I saw enough. Now, do not be suspecting me of a pun, I entreat.'

In November, Jane wrote to her niece Fanny with advice about a troublesome love affair: 'Anything is to be preferred or endured rather than marrying without Affection.'[85] Her letter revealed that she was as keen as any modern-day author for her latest book to sell well: 'People are more ready to borrow & praise, than to buy

– which I cannot wonder at, but tho' I like praise as well as anybody, I like what Edward calls *Pewter* too.'[86] Before signing off, she reported that the first edition of *Mansfield Park* had already sold out. 'Your Uncle Henry is rather wanting me to come to Town, to settle about a 2nd Edit … I am very greedy & want to make the most of it.' *Mansfield Park* was her most successful novel in terms of financial return, with the invested profits giving her an income of around £30 a year.

Unaccountably, however, Thomas Egerton refused to print a second edition. He was also prevaricating over the publication of *Emma*. Jane wrote the novel between January 1814 and March 1815, whilst making regular trips to London to see Henry and looking after a constant stream of visiting relatives at Chawton. The time had come for Jane to find a new publisher. Henry duly offered *Emma* to John Murray of Albermarle Street. Happily, Murray agreed to publish it, along with that hitherto elusive second edition of *Mansfield Park*. Henry had done well to secure the services of John Murray, the most celebrated and influential publisher of the day. His authors included Sir Walter Scott, George Crabbe and, most notoriously, Lord Byron, who had become his close friend and correspondent. Three years previously, in 1812, Murray had published Byron's second book, *Childe Harold's Pilgrimage*. It had sold out in five days, leading Byron to remark, 'I awoke one morning and found myself famous.' After Byron's death in 1824, Murray burnt the poet's memoirs in the fireplace of his office, in order to protect his reputation.

The most prominent publisher of the day he may have been, but John Murray still tried to pull a fast one on the lady author from Hampshire. 'Mr Murray's Letter is come; he is a Rogue of course, but a civil one,' wrote Jane to Cassandra in October 1815.[87] Murray had offered £450 to publish *Emma* but wanted the copyrights of *Mansfield Park* and *Sense and Sensibility* thrown in as well. Jane was roused and charmed at the same time: 'It will end in my publishing for myself I dare say. – He sends more praise however than I expected. It is an amusing Letter.'

Then Henry became ill with a bilious fever. An apothecary took 20 ounces of blood from his patient each day, while Jane dispensed 'Medicine, Tea and Barley Water'. Henry managed to dictate a reply to John Murray, refusing the publisher's offer on behalf of his sister: 'The Terms you offer are so very inferior to what we had expected, that I am apprehensive of having made some great Error in my Arithmetical Calculation.'[88] Henry's continuing bout of illness eventually forced Jane to tackle John Murray herself, and she wrote to him in early November, 'desirous of coming to some decision on the affair in question', and asking him to call at Henry's house in Hans Place.[89] She eventually settled for publication of *Emma* on commission, with Murray to keep 10 per cent of the profits.

One of the doctors called in to attend Henry, Dr Baillie, was also a physician at the royal court. He told Jane that the Prince Regent was an admirer of her work. Jane was certainly no admirer of the Prince, partly on account of his marital shenanigans. Of his estranged wife, Princess Caroline, she had once written: 'I shall support her as long as I can because she is a Woman, and because I hate her Husband.'[90] But when the Prince's librarian, James Stanier Clarke, called on Jane and invited her to visit the library at Carlton House, the Regent's luxurious London residence in St James's, she went. Then Stanier hinted that she might like to dedicate her next book to the Prince. This was tantamount to a royal command. *Emma* duly came out early in 1816, fronted by a flourish to the Prince: 'To His Royal Highness The Prince Regent, This work is by His Royal Highness's Permission, most respectfully dedicated, by his Royal Highness's dutiful and obedient humble servant, The Author.' The Prince's thoughts on *Emma*, if any, are not known. However, John Murray printed 2,000 copies – the largest print run of any of Jane's novels to date – and charged 21 shillings for the three volumes.

After the muted reception *Mansfield Park* had received, Jane was worried about what her audience would make of her latest novel, as a letter to James Stanier Clarke written in December 1815 reveals:

My greatest anxiety at present is that this 4th work should not disgrace what was good in the others. But on this point I will do myself the justice to declare that whatever may be my wishes for its' [*sic*] success, I am very strongly haunted by the idea that to those Readers who have preferred P&P it will appear inferior in Wit, & to those who have preferred MP very inferior in good Sense. Such as it is however, I hope you will do me the favour of accepting a Copy.[91]

When he read *Emma*, Jane's nephew Edward pointed out a rare continuity error in his aunt's work: she had made Mr Knightley's apple trees blossom in July. Despite this slip up, many readers rate *Emma* as Jane's most accomplished novel, discerning elements of a detective story in its intricate construction. She famously said that she was going to take 'a heroine whom no-one but myself will much like': the handsome, clever and rich Emma Woodhouse. Possessed, unlike all her previous heroines, of all possible advantages, Emma proceeds to make rather a mess of things, remaining blithely blind to everything she does not want to see, until finally she listens to the advice of the one man in her life she belatedly realises she cannot do without.

By the time *Emma* came out, Henry had recovered from his illness and Jane was back in Chawton. She was never to visit London again. A few months later, Henry's bank failed and he went bankrupt. Eliza having died in the spring of 1813, he decided that he had enough of the financial world and of the City. Soon afterwards he took Holy Orders and went to live in Chawton near his sisters.

At the beginning of 1816, Jane, who had recently turned 40, began to feel unwell. Her symptoms included pain, severe fatigue and discolouration of the skin. At first, ill health did not prevent her from working harder than ever. She finally retrieved the manuscript of *Susan* from Thomas Crosby for the £10 she had paid for it and began to rework it a little, changing the name of her heroine from Susan to Catherine. The previous summer she had begun writing her final completed novel, *Persuasion* – known to its author as *The Elliots* – finishing it a year later in July 1816. She laboured particularly hard to get the ending right, completing the first draft but then quickly becoming dissatisfied with the tone of the two concluding chapters. James Edward Austen-Leigh recalled in *A Memoir of Jane Austen* that, when she had finished the novel:

> her performance did not satisfy her. She thought it tame and flat, and was desirous of producing something better. This weighed upon her mind, the more so probably on account of the weak state of her health; so that one night she retired to rest in very low spirits.

But such depression was little in accordance with her nature, and was soon shaken off. The next morning she awoke to more cheerful views and brighter inspirations; the sense of power revived; and imaginations resumed its course. She cancelled the condemned chapter, and wrote two others, entirely different in its stead.

The discarded chapters are the only surviving portion of original manuscript from Jane's completed novels and are now in the British Library. The chapters which replace them are among the most moving in all her novels, as the estranged lovers finally find each other again without actually speaking. 'You pierce my soul,' writes Captain Wentworth to Anne Elliot. 'I am half agony, half hope. Tell me not that I am too late, that such precious feelings are gone for ever.' In March 1817, Jane wrote to her niece Fanny:

Miss Catherine is put upon the Shelve for the present, and I do not know that she will ever come out; – but I have something ready for Publication, which may perhaps appear about a twelvemonth hence … You may *perhaps* like the heroine, as she is almost too good for me.[92]

*Persuasio*n did appear, but not in Jane Austen's lifetime. It was published by John Murray at the very end of 1817, together with *Miss Catherine* (retitled *Northanger Abbey*) in a four-volume set. In his 'Biographical Notice of the Author' which prefaced the two novels, Henry Austen attempted to explain the delay in their publication: 'Though in composition she was equally rapid and correct, yet an invincible distrust of her own judgement induced her to withhold her works from the public, till time and many perusals had satisfied her that the charm of recent composition was dissolved.' *Persuasion* is the most sombre and bittersweet of Jane's novels. By contrast with the others, where her lovers come together in a relatively short time, it is eight long years before the misunderstandings between Captain Wentworth and Anne Elliot are finally resolved. 'All the privilege I claim for my own sex', cries Anne at the end of the novel, 'is that of loving longest, when existence or when hope is gone.'

Jane's letters from Chawton throughout 1816 remained unfailingly cheerful. On the domestic front there was rarely a lull: Chawton Cottage was alive with the larks of Jane's many nieces and nephews. She was now a great-aunt too, after the birth late the previous summer of Anna-Jemima, a daughter to her niece, Anna. But despite the liveliness of the company, Jane's health failed to improve. In May 1816, she and Cassandra went to take the spa waters at Cheltenham in the hope of alleviating the symptoms of her illness. In July 1816, she finished *Persuasion* and put the manuscript aside. Only in September did her letters begin to hint that all was not well. 'Thank you, my Back has given me scarcely any pain for many days,' Jane wrote to Cassandra, who had returned to Cheltenham with Mary, their brother James' wife.[93] 'I am nursing myself up now into as beautiful a state as I can.' In December, Jane disclosed in a letter to her nephew James Edward that she had declined an invitation to dine with Anna at nearby Wyards Farm: 'The walk is beyond my strength (though I am otherwise very well).'[94] In January 1817, she declared that she was 'getting stronger than I was half a year ago, & can so perfectly well walk to Alton, or back again, without that slightest fatigue that I hope to be able to do both when Summer comes'.[95]

This brief reprieve from her symptoms gave her the energy to begin a new novel, *Sanditon*. Ironically, and perhaps appropriately, this unfinished novel is a sharp satire on hypochondria, in which Jane pokes merciless fun at those who obsess about their health. It is set in the small village of Sanditon, which is being developed into a seaside resort. Mr Parker, one of the prime movers behind the development, has two sisters, Diana and Susan, of whom he remarks, 'I do not believe they know what a day's health is', together with a younger brother, Arthur, who is 'so delicate he can engage in no profession'.

At first it seems that all three siblings will be too ill to travel to Sanditon. Diana feels that the sea will probably be the 'death' of her, afflicted as she is by her 'old grievance' which has left her 'hardly able to crawl from her bed to the sofa'. Susan, meanwhile, having endured six leeches a day for ten days to no avail, has been persuaded by her sister that the cause of her headache lies in her gums and so has had three teeth drawn. Now she can 'only speak in a whisper' and faints away twice 'on poor Arthur's trying to suppress a cough'. Arthur himself is 'tolerably well', but 'Diana fears for his liver'.

Eventually they make it to Sanditon, reasonably unscathed by the journey. Even Susan has no 'hysterics of consequence' until they have all but arrived. The book's heroine, the eminently sensible Charlotte Heywood, observes the visitors' strange habits and ailments, and concludes that they have no symptoms which 'she would not have undertaken to cure, by putting out the fire, opening the window, and disposing of the drops and salts by means of one or the other'.

It is clear that Jane had little patience with illness. 'Sickness,' she wrote to her niece Fanny Knight, 'is a dangerous Indulgence at my time of Life.'[96] She wanted to be busy; to be useful to her nieces and nephews; to be writing. In *Sanditon*, the delusion of ill health is parodied as the consequence of an idle mind: 'Disorders and recoveries so very much out of the common way, seemed more like the amusement of eager minds in want of employment than of actual afflictions and relief.' It's almost as if Jane believed she could write away her own illness by satirising those who languish on sofas. Her brother Henry later wrote that she supported 'all the varying pain, irksomeness, and tedium attendant on decaying nature ... with a truly elastic cheerfulness'.[97]

But despite her best efforts of mind, Jane's own health refused to comply and her symptoms continued to worsen. In March 1817, even *Sanditon* was put aside, to remain uncompleted. The fate Jane had in mind for her entertaining trio of '*malades imaginaires*' will forever remain a mystery. But there was nothing imaginary about her own symptoms. By early April, after a bilious attack and fever, Jane admitted to having felt 'too unwell this last fortnight to write anything that was not absolutely necessary'.[98] On 27 April, she penned her Last Will and Testament, leaving everything to Cassandra apart from a legacy of £50 to Henry. In a compassionate gesture, she also left the same amount to his former cook, Mme Bigeon, who had lost everything when Henry's bank had gone bust the previous year.

A few days after making her will, it was agreed that Jane should travel the 16 miles from Chawton to Winchester. The hospital there had an excellent reputation and Jane was to be under the direct care of one of its 'capital surgeons', Giles King Lyford, who had already treated her with some success. Describing herself in a letter to Anne Sharp, the former governess at Godmersham, as 'a very genteel, portable sort of an Invalid', she set off on

24 May in her brother Edward's carriage, accompanied by Cassandra, and with her brother Henry and nephew William riding alongside in the rain for most of the way.[99]

Lodged in a house in College Street, Jane managed, now and again during the day, to walk from room to room, but mostly she stayed on the sofa, in a cruel echo of the gloriously indolent Diana Parker in *Sanditon*. She was only able to go outside once in a sedan chair, but hoped that when the weather improved she might be 'promoted to a wheel-chair'.[100] It was not to be. In the early hours of 18 July 1817, Jane Austen died in her sister Cassandra's arms. She was 41 years old.

'She felt herself to be dying about half and hour before she became tranquil & aparently [*sic*] unconscious,' wrote Cassandra to their niece Fanny, two days after Jane's death.[101] 'When I asked her if there was any thing she wanted, her answer was she wanted nothing but death & some of her words were "God grant me patience. Pray for me, Oh Pray for me."' Then Cassandra added, 'She was the sun of my life, the gilder of every pleasure, the soother of every sorrow.'

Jane Austen's funeral took place at Winchester Cathedral on the following Thursday 24 July. The fact that the Austens were a clerical family seems to have ensured that there was no difficulty in getting permission for Jane to be buried in such a hallowed location, and a vault was made ready in the north aisle of the cathedral. Meanwhile,

Jane's body lay in an open coffin in the dining room at College Street. 'Even now,' wrote Cassandra, gazing upon her dead sister, 'there is such a sweet serene air over her countenance as is quite pleasant to contemplate.'[102]

Jane's funeral was scheduled for an early hour so as not to disrupt the schedule of daily services in the cathedral. The cortege consisted of her brothers, Edward, Henry and Frank, and her nephew, James Edward, who rode over from Steventon. It was not customary for women to attend funerals in the early nineteenth century, so Cassandra stayed away. She 'watched the little mournful procession the length of the street & and when it turned from my sight I had lost her forever'.[103] A few days later, she returned alone to Chawton.

What did Jane Austen die of? The little that is known of her symptoms has traditionally led to a diagnosis of Addison's Disease, a rare condition, only recognised some decades later, which is brought about when the adrenal glands do not make enough cortisol, the steroid hormone which regulates blood pressure and the immune system. More recently there have been plausible suggestions that she may have died of a lymphoma such as Hodgkin's Disease.

Jane Austen was the seventh of eight children, and the first of them to die. With the exception of her eldest brother James, who died in 1819, aged 54, the Austens were a long-lived family. Jane's mother, who appears to have been something of a hypochondriac, lived to 87, and six of her siblings, including Cassandra, lived well into their seventies or eighties. Jane's last surviving sibling was Frank Austen – Admiral Frank Austen, as he became – who died aged 91 in 1865. We can only speculate what wonderful writing would have come from Jane's pen had she lived to a similarly ripe age.

6

The Global Celebrity
1817–Present

Pity Jane Austen if you must, this maiden lady without children or sexual experience. But she would have known the exhilaration of the writer when she put down her pen after 'Pride & Prejudice'. I bet she knew that what she'd written would outrun the generations.

Fay Weldon, 1999[104]

In 1926, Rudyard Kipling wrote some verses in praise of Jane Austen:

> Jane lies in Winchester – blessed be her shade!
> Praise the Lord for making her, and for all she made!
> And while the stones of Winchester, or Milsom Street, remain
> Glory, love and honour unto England's Jane![105]

So why, when so much now separates our modern world from hers, are we still so in thrall to 'England's Jane'?

Published with only limited success in her own short lifetime, Jane Austen's novels have had the most extraordinary afterlife. Two hundred years later, her portraits of the lives of '3 or 4 Families in a Country Village' have indeed 'outrun the generations' and are revered by readers across the world: as classic literature worthy of deep study; as vivid portrayals of human relationships; as 'boy meets girl – girl gets boy' romances; as authentic period pieces evoking an apparently simpler existence for which we are incurably nostalgic.

At first, posthumous fame came slowly. The memorial description on Jane's black marble gravestone in Winchester Cathedral famously makes no mention of her writing, but praises only 'the benevolence of her heart, the sweetness of her temper and the extraordinary endowments of her mind'. Though Henry's biographical note of 1817 in the first combined editions of *Persuasion* and *Northanger Abbey* finally revealed his sister's identity to the public at large, it wasn't long before all her novels fell out of print. In 1832, Jane's family sold the five copyrights they still held to publisher Richard Bentley for £210. And that, it seemed, would be that; especially in an age characterised by the huge popularity of other, rather different novelists: Charles Dickens, William Makepeace Thackeray and Wilkie Collins. Lord Tennyson was an admirer of Jane's work but that novelist of the great Yorkshire outdoors, Charlotte Brontë, was not, remarking that she would 'hardly like to live with her ladies and gentlemen, in their elegant, confined houses'.[106]

But gradually, some celebrated fans of Jane Austen's work began to make their voices heard. Sir Walter Scott was one of the earliest. After reading *Pride and Prejudice* for the third time in 1826, he wrote in his diary: 'That young lady had a talent for describing the involvement and feelings and characters of ordinary life which is to me the most wonderful I ever met with.'[107] Interest in Jane Austen's novels was further revived a few decades later by the publication of her nephew James Edward's *Memoir of Jane Austen* in 1870. It sold well and, in 1872, he used some of the proceeds to erect a brass plaque in the aisle of Winchester Cathedral, which finally distinguished his aunt as 'Jane Austen ... known to many by her writings'. Richard Bentley reissued all Jane's novels in 1870, followed by a deluxe collected edition in 1882. The following year, an undergraduate student at Harvard wrote the first known dissertation on her novels and won a prize for it.

Austen's growing popularity also owed something to her increasing reputation as the most quintessentially English novelist: 'England's Jane', as Rudyard Kipling called her. He was a confirmed fan and even wrote a story entitled 'The Janeites' about a group of First World War soldiers who are secret admirers of her work. The story was partly inspired by the fact that Jane's novels were widely used during that conflict as aids to recovery for wounded and severely shell-shocked troops in military hospitals.

In 1940 came the first film version of one of Jane Austen's novels, with the release of *Pride and Prejudice* starring Greer Garson and Laurence Olivier in a screen adaptation by Aldous Huxley. The Jane Austen Society was formed during the Second World War, when no less a figure than Winston Churchill had *Pride and Prejudice* read aloud to him by his daughter Sarah while he was recovering from pneumonia. 'What calm lives they had, those people!' he wrote later. 'No worries about the French Revolution, or the crashing struggle of the Napoleonic Wars.'[108]

It cannot be denied that Jane's stories are set in places which epitomise the green and pleasant land; that rosy view of England still treasured, both at home and abroad. In our uncertain world, the books she wrote stand for many as conservative symbols of the things they most value. The film and TV adaptations of her work have also helped promote the view that in Jane's time life was simpler and more graceful; tea was always served in china cups on a clean tablecloth; women wore elegant dresses and men bowed low. Her romances are often marketed in gentle pastel covers to appeal to those who want to cushion themselves within a story of yesteryear that has a happy ending.

This chintzy version of 'England's Jane' completely fails to go the distance in explaining her enduring and international popularity, however. If Jane's 'Englishness' is the key to the appeal of her work then why have her books been translated into numerous languages across the globe? How does it explain the Bollywood version of her novel, *Bride & Prejudice*, or *Clueless* – a film which sets *Emma* in a modern-day Beverley Hills high school?

Jane Austen, 'heritage icon', has come to stand for a way of life which she herself would hardly recognise. Her days were not spent doing needlework or simpering at men in velvet tailcoats. She was an acerbic, driven woman who loved a party, but had no trouble being alone, particularly if she had a pen in her hand. And though she famously never found love, she enjoyed, for a few short years, something she prized much more highly: the rare thrill – especially for a woman of that time – of seeing her writing in print.

Not only has Jane Austen's work scarcely been out of print since; her novels are now regarded by academics the world over as marking an important watershed in the development of English literature. They are the first truly modern novels in which the structure of prose narrative is elevated to an art form. As John Mullan, Professor of English Literature at University College London, puts it, Jane Austen's 'fearless innovations ... taught later novelists to filter narration through the minds of their own characters ... Austen gave her readers an entirely new sense of a person's inner life'.[109]

And yet, none of this greatness was ever acknowledged or even imagined in Jane Austen's own lifetime. An amusing comic strip by the cartoonist Posy Simmonds pictures Jane contemplating a journey forward into our own times, to bask in the worldwide adoration which she never had the chance to experience. 'Jane! Jane! Come on Over! The Nation has voted! You are the Number One Pillar of English Lit! ... You're a Celebrity ... get yourself over here,' shouts a TV presenter in the first frame.[110] Jane almost crosses the Stygian divide to receive the laurels and fanfares. Suddenly, however, the prospect of having to answer impertinent twenty-first-century questions about the number of sexual partners she has had, the ecological effects of writing on little bits of ivory and her opinion of Colin Firth's tight breeches convince her that it would be better to remain in her own era.

In one sense, Posy Simmonds has it right. Any attempt to drag Jane Austen over to the twenty-first century side is doomed to failure. Her world was quite different, and bringing modern-day sensibilities and interpretations to her work risks muddying her genius. In *Recreating Jane Austen*, John Wiltshire writes, 'Every cultural creation, even a cathedral, has an afterlife, unpredictable, uncontrolled by its original architect, when another era, another cultural configuration turns it, adapts it to its own use.' Wiltshire confronts those who still think Jane Austen created a world that is 'far-off, impeccably gracious and morally superannuated'. Actually, he says, we have in Jane a novelist who is 'sassy, spunky, post-colonial, radical, transgressive, sexually complex and ambiguous'.

In short, the remarkable, enduring popularity of Jane Austen's novels shows that there are qualities in her writing which make it both universally resonant and appropriate for any era. Her books can be read on myriad levels, and they can be read merely for pleasure. That is the secret of their success. As Claire Harman remarks at the end of her perceptive book, *Jane's Fame: How Jane*

Austen Conquered the World, 'it is impossible to imagine a time when she or her works could have delighted us long enough'.

In a letter to Cassandra in January 1796, years before she had any glimmer of being a published writer, Jane Austen declared that she wrote 'only for Fame, and without any view to pecuniary Emolument'.[111] She achieved neither in her lifetime, but her fame would one day be great indeed. In fact, it would be giant.

Notes

1   Quoted in *The Guardian*, 11 May 1999.
2   Le Faye, Deirdre (ed.), *Jane's Austen's Letters* (Oxford University Press, 1997), p. 312.
3   Ibid., p. 275.
4   *The Journal of Sir Walter Scott*, March 1826 (Cambridge University Press, 2013).
5   Quoted in Southam, Brian, *Jane Austen: The Critical Heritage* (Routledge, 1968).
6   Introduction to *Love and Freindship*, by G.K. Chesterton (1922) (HarperPerennial Classics, 2012).
7   *Jane Austen's Letters*, op. cit., p. 31.
8   Ibid., p. 26.
9   Ibid., p. 17.
10 Ibid., p. 29.
11 Ibid., p. 35.
12 Ibid., p. 61.
13 Ibid., p. 17.
14 Bibliographical Notice of the Author, Preface to *Persuasion and Northanger Abbey*, by Henry Austen (Richard Bentley, 1818).

15 *Jane Austen's Letters*, op. cit., p. 26.

16 Austen-Leigh, James Edward, *A Memoir of Jane Austen and Other Family Recollections* (Richard Bentley, 1870).

17 Introduction to *Love and Freindship*, op. cit.

18 James, P.D., *Time to be in Earnest: A Fragment of Autobiography* (Faber, 1999).

19 *Jane Austen's Letters*, op. cit., p. 2.

20 Ibid., p. 4.

21 Ibid., p. 4.

22 Ibid., p. 35.

23 Letter to Millie Warne, Beatrix Potter, 1905.

24 Nicolson, Nigel, *Was Jane Austen Happy in Bath?* (Holborne Museum of Art, 2002), p. 6.

25 *Jane Austen's Letters*, op. cit., p. 66.

26 Ibid., p. 68.

27 Ibid., p. 30.

28 Ibid., p. 39.

29 Ibid., p. 41.

30 Ibid., p. 76.

31 Ibid., p. 44.

32 Ibid., p. 46.

33 Ibid., p. 67.

34 Ibid., p. 83.

35 Ibid., p. 82.

36 Ibid., p. 85.

37 Ibid., p. 85.

38   Ibid., p. 96.

39   Ibid., p. 67.

40   Ibid., p. 138.

41   Piece for *The Times Literary Supplement*, 8 May 1913.

42   *Jane Austen's Letters*, op. cit., p. 114.

43   Ibid., p. 117.

44   Ibid., p. 123.

45   *A Memoir of Jane Austen*, op. cit.

46   Letter from Fanny Knight Knatchbull to her sister Marianne, 1869.

47   *Jane Austen's Letters*, op. cit., p. 108.

48   Ibid., p. 139.

49   Ibid., p. 137.

50   Ibid., p. 249.

51   Quoted in Hill, Constance, *Jane Austen: Her Homes and Her Friends* (John Lane, 1902).

52   *Jane Austen's Letters*, op. cit., p. 127.

53   Ibid., p. 346.

54   Ibid., p. 107.

55   Ibid., p. 234.

56   Ibid., p. 237.

57   Ibid., p. 12.

58   Ibid., p. 126.

59   Ibid., p. 135.

60   Ibid., p. 139.

61   Ibid., p. 149.

62   Ibid., p. 140.

63   Ibid., p. 119.

64   Ibid., p. 156.

65   Ibid., p. 156.

66   Ibid., p. 174.

67   Ibid., p. 175.

68   Quoted in *O, The Oprah Magazine*, January 2001.

69   *Jane Austen's Letters*, op. cit., p. 175.

70   Ibid., p. 316.

71   Ibid., p. 321.

72   Ibid, pp. 179, 182.

73   Quoted in Harman, Claire, *Jane's Fame: How Jane Austen Conquered the World* (Canongate, 2009), p. 53.

74   Ibid., p. 197.

75   Ibid., p. 201.

76   Ibid., p. 205.

77   Quoted in *Jane's Fame*, op. cit.

78   Quoted in *Jane Austen: The Critical Heritage*, op. cit.

79   *Jane Austen's Letters*, op. cit., p. 201.

80   Ibid., p. 217.

81   Ibid., p. 231.

82   Austen-Leigh, M.A., *Personal Aspects of Jane Austen* (1920).

83   Ibid., pp. 268, 275.

84   In 'Opinions of Mansfield Park', collected by Jane Austen, in British Library. First published in

abridged form in the first edition of *A Memoir of Jane Austen*, op. cit. See also http://www.janeausten. ac.uk/edition/ms/OpinionsHeadNote.html.

85 Ibid., p. 280.

86 Ibid., p. 287.

87 Ibid., p. 291.

88 Ibid., p. 293.

89 Ibid., p. 295.

90 Ibid., p. 208.

91 Ibid., p. 306.

92 Ibid., p. 333.

93 Ibid., p. 320.

94 Ibid., p. 323.

95 Ibid., p. 326.

96 Ibid., p. 336.

97 Bibliographical Notice of the Author, Preface to *Persuasion and Northanger Abbey*, op. cit.

98 *Jane Austen's Letters*, op. cit., p. 338.

99 Ibid., p. 340.

100 Ibid., p. 343.

101 Ibid., p. 344.

102 Ibid., p. 345.

103 Ibid., p. 347.

104 *The Sunday Times*, 17 October 1999.

105 Epigraph to 'The Janenites', by Rudyard Kipling, in *Debits and Credits* (1926).

106 Letter to G.H. Lewes, 1848.

107 *The Journal of Sir Walter Scott*, op. cit., note 4.

108 Churchill, Winston, *The Second World War*, Vol. 5 (1952).

109 Mullan, John, *What Matters in Jane Austen?* (Bloomsbury, 2012).

110 Simmonds, Posy, in *Literary Life*, 2003.

111 *Jane Austen's Letters*, op. cit., p. 3.

Timeline

1775	Born on 16 December, Steventon, Hampshire
1783	Sent to school in Oxford, then Southampton
1785	Short stay at school in Reading
1790	Writes *Love and Freindship* (*sic*)
1791	Writes *The History of England*
1792	Writes *Lesley Castle*
1794	Writes *Lady Susan*
1795	Writes *Elinor and Marianne* (later *Sense and Sensibility*)
1796–97	Writes *First Impressions* (later *Pride and Prejudice*)
1797	*First Impressions* rejected by publisher Thomas Cadell
1798	Writes *Susan* (later *Northanger Abbey*)
1801	Rev. George Austen retires Austen family moves to Bath
1802	Accepts then rejects a marriage proposal from Harris Bigg-Wither
1803	Revised version of *Susan* sold to publisher Richard Crosby for £10

1804	Begins writing *The Watsons*
1805	Rev. George Austen dies
1806	Moves to Southampton
1809	Moves to Chawton, Hampshire
	Manuscript of *Susan* returned, unpublished
	Revises *Sense and Sensibility*
1810	*Sense and Sensibility* accepted for publication by publisher Thomas Egerton
1811	*Sense and Sensibility* published
	Begins writing *Mansfield Park*
1812	*Pride and Prejudice* sold to Thomas Egerton for £110
1813	*Pride and Prejudice* published
	Mansfield Park completed
1814	*Mansfield Park* published
	Begins writing *Emma*
1816	*Emma* published by John Murray
	Revises *Susan* and retitles it *Northanger Abbey*
	The Elliots (later *Persuasion*) completed
1817	Begins writing *Sanditon*
	Dies 18 July and buried in Winchester Cathedral
1818	*Northanger Abbey* and *Persuasion* posthumously published

Further Reading

Austen-Leigh, J.E., *A Memoir of Jane Austen and Other Family Recollections* (Richard Bentley, 1870)

Byrne, Paula, *The Real Jane Austen: A Life in Small Things* (HarperPress, 2013)

Harman, Claire, *Jane's Fame: How Jane Austen Conquered the World* (Canongate, 2009)

Hill, Constance, *Jane Austen: Her Home, Her Friends* (John Lane, 1902)

Lane, Maggie & Selwyn, David (eds), *Jane Austen: A Celebration* (Carcanet, 2000)

Le Faye, Deirdre (ed.), *Jane's Austen's Letters* (Oxford University Press, 1997)

Le Faye, Deirdre, *Jane Austen: The World of Her Novels* (Frances Lincoln, 2003)

Mullan, John, *What Matters in Jane Austen?* (Bloomsbury, 2012)

Nicolson, Nigel, *Was Jane Austen Happy in Bath?* (Holborne Museum of Art, 2002)

Nokes, David, *Jane Austen: A Life* (Fourth Estate, 1997)

Sanderson, Caroline, *A Rambling Fancy: In the Footsteps of Jane Austen* (Cadogan, 2006)

Shields, Carol, *Jane Austen* (Weidenfeld, 2001)

Southam, Brian, *Jane Austen: The Critical Heritage* (Routledge, 1968)

Tomalin, Claire, *Jane Austen: A Life* (Viking, 1997)

Wiltshire, John, *Recreating Jane Austen* (Cambridge University Press, 2001)

Web Links

There are many online resources available for those wanting to find out more about Jane Austen and her work. Here are some of the most useful:

www.janeausten.ac.uk/index.html – Jane Austen's Fiction Manuscripts Digital Edition gathers together in the virtual space of the web some 1,100 pages of fiction written in Jane Austen's own hand
www.janeausten.co.uk – Website of the Jane Austen Centre in Bath
www.jane-austens-house-museum.org.uk – Website of the Jane Austen House Museum in Chawton, Hampshire
www.janeaustensoci.freeuk.com – Website of the Jane Austen Society of the UK
www.jasna.org – Website of the Jane Austen Society of North America
www.pemberley.com – 'A haven for Jane Austen addicts'
www.seekingjaneausten.com – A guide to the locations associated with Jane Austen

Acknowledgements

Thank you to: my mother Margaret, whose school prize copy of *Pride and Prejudice* was the start of it. And my discerning daughter Julia who is Jane Austen's latest fan.

Giuseppe Verdi Henry V **Brunel** Pope John Paul II **Jane Austen** William the Conqueror **Abraham Lincoln** Robert the Bruce **Charles Darwin** Buddha **Elizabeth I** Horatio Nelson **Wellington** Hannibal & Scipio **Jesus** Joan of Arc **Anne Frank** Alfred the Great **King Arthur** Henry Ford **Nelson Mandela**